Longman Handbooks for Language Teachers

Christopher Jones and Sue Fortescue

Using Computers in the Language Classroom

Consultant Editors: Neville Grant and Jeremy Harmer

Longman

London and New York

Longman Group UK Limited
Longman House, Burnt Mill, Harlow,
Essex CM20 2JE, England
and Associated Companies throughout the world.

Distributed in the United States of America by Longman Publishing, New York

First published 1987

Third impression 1991

BRITISH LIBRARY CATALOGUING IN PUBLICATION DATA
Jones, Christopher
    Using computers in the language classroom.
    (Longman handbooks for language teachers)
    1. Language and languages — Computer assisted instruction
    I. Title   II. Fortescue, Susan 407'.8   P53

ISBN 0-582-74617-5

LIBRARY OF CONGRESS CATALOGING IN PUBLICATION DATA
Jones, Christopher
    Using computers in the language classroom.
    (Longman handbooks for language teachers)
    Bibliography: p.
    Includes index.
    1. Language and languages — Computer-assisted instruction   I. Fortesceu, Susan.
II. Title   III. Series.
P53.28.J66   1986   418'.028'5   86-7201
ISBN 0-582-74617-5

Produced by Longman Singapore Publishers Pte Ltd
Printed in Singapore

ACKNOWLEDGEMENTS
Too many people have helped either directly or indirectly in the creation of this book for us
to thank them all by name. Our grateful thanks for a collective wealth of ideas are due to
Michael Carrier, Graham Davies, David Eastment, Jeremy Fox, Frank Heyworth, John
Higgins, Tim Johns, Michael Johnson, Glyn Jones, Alison Piper, Peter Roach, Damien
Tunnacliffe, Marjorie Vai and Tony Williams. Thanks also to the principal, staff and students
of Eurocentre Bournemouth, and to our editor, Louise Elkins.

We are grateful to the following for permission to reproduce copyright material:
Acornsoft Limited for page 67 (left); Amstrad for page 107 (bottom left and right); Apple
Computer U.K. Limited for page 107 (middle right); BBC CEEFAX for page 58 (top left
and right); Bourne Educational for page 22; Reproduced from Yellow River Kingdom from
the BBC Welcome Pack with the permission of the British Broadcasting Corporation for
page 63 (left and right); Beebugsoft Limited for page 86 (bottom); Bell College, Saffron
Walden for page 58 (bottom left and right); Programs designed and developed by the British
Council and published by Cambridge University Press for page 66 (right), 75 (top left and
right); Camsoft for page 19 (top left, right and bottom), 38 (bottom left); CBS for page 75
(bottom left and right); Computer Concepts for page 50 (bottom), 51 (left and right); Willis
Edmonson, University of Hamburg for page 62; Eurocentre, Bournemouth for page 2, 122
(bottom); Eurocentre, Cambridge for page 50 (top), 122 (top); Jeremy Fox, University of
East Anglia for page 33; Heinemann Educational Books Limited (The Dudley Programs,
Five Ways Software) for page 30 (right); John Higgins for page 18 (top left, right and
bottom), 94 (top left, right and bottom); IBM UK Limited for page 107 (top right); Tim
Johns for page 23 (left and right), 91 (left and right); Glyn Jones, Davies's School of English,
for page 16, 82 (left and right); Josephine Jones for page 31; Michael Johnson for page 30
(left); Minnesota Educational Computing Corporation for page 67 (right); Oxford University
Press for page 34 (left); Psion Software for page 27 (right); Sierra On-Line for page 70;
Simon W. Hessel Software for page 66 (left); VIFI: Nathan for page 17; Universal Press
Syndicate © 1982 G.B. Trudeau for page facing page 1, and page 137; Wida Software
Limited for pages 10, 11 (left and right), 23 (bottom), 26 (top left and right, bottom left and
right); 27 (left), 38 (top left and bottom right), 39 (top left and right), 39 (middle left and
right), 39 (bottom), 42, 43, 46 (top left and right, bottom left and right, 86 (top left and
right).
The photographs on pages 3, 107 (top and middle left), 136 (permission Eurocentre,
Bournemouth), are by the Longman Photo Unit.

Contents

Foreword

Doonesbury   by Garry Trudeau

This cartoon will strike a chord with many language teachers who have wondered whether computers might help their students to learn a language. As often as not, their enquiries are met with a stream of jargon that will deter all but the most resolute.

Most language teachers do not wish to become computer scientists. Rather, they want to know how computers can help in the everyday business of language learning, in areas like grammar, writing, speaking, listening, reading and vocabulary; what kinds of activities can be conducted around a computer keyboard; whether computers can be used by groups in class as well as by individuals in self-access. Only if they find satisfactory answers to these questions will they need to know what machines to buy, how to operate them, and, maybe, how to write programs.

This book aims to show what teachers and learners can do with computers in the language classroom. Starting with categories that are familiar to language teachers, it describes the kinds of classroom activities that take place every day in schools where computers are in use, and tries to show the relevance of those activities to the language learner. It also gives practical advice to those who wish to begin using computers in their own schools.

Above all, it aims to be a user-friendly guide to computer-assisted language learning, rather than a language-teacher-compatible paper-based random-access information retrieval system.

Introduction

Tony Williams, Director, Wida Software

In 1987, the year that this book was first published, Professor Dieter Wolff, then of Düsseldorf University, made a tour of the United Kingdom to gather information on innovative programs in the use of computers in language teaching — and found nothing essentially new. The explosion of creative thought in CALL that marked the early 1980s had seemingly fizzled out and we were now entering a period of consolidation. With certain notable exceptions, this finding still holds good.

By 1990 computers had established themselves firmly in language schools throughout the world, and some CALL experience, for instance, is increasingly a requisite qualification for new appointees at college language departments; new language centres are almost inconceivable without a CALL component. This book has played a key historical role in the process of getting CALL accepted. It has often been distributed to trainees as part of CALL introductory courses.

Although much has happened in the world of technology since it was written, the relevance of the teaching practices described in Christopher Jones and Sue Fortescue's book and the ideas and possibilities they explore has not been diminished. For this reason the main body of the book has been left intact, and changes have been wholly confined to the appendices.

Significantly we have felt able to pare down the glossary to terms specific to CALL. The computer has established such a place for itself in teaching that much of its jargon ('input', 'BASIC', etc.) has become common parlance and is best left to computer familiarisation courses for the beginner.

There has been an unmistakable shift over to IBM-compatible machines in education almost everywhere in the world, strongly challenged, however, by the Apple Macintosh especially in the USA and Australia. These developments have been highly beneficial in that they have set common standards of keyboard conventions and software availability. Language teachers can now go to other countries, buy applications software, games, text adventures in other languages and use them, unmodified, on the computers in their own schools. Consequently the rewritten appendices reflect the growth of IBM and Macintosh applications and place less emphasis on British software and more on European and American language programs.

Computer Assisted Language Learning has become a mass phenomenon and the techniques traditionally associated with it are used in tens of thousands of the most varied institutions, from primary schools, to prisons, hospitals, universities and companies. CALL is still largely in the hands of the enthusiastic individual teacher, however, and only rarely is it part of a larger team effort. But even here things are on the move and the many open access learning centres coming into existence are ensuring continuity by establishing collective evaluation and development practices.

While the 'language industries' on the one hand can command the massive resources to make effective use of the latest expensive technology, laser disks, on-line data bases, compact disk storage, interactive video, satellite communication and the like, language schools on the other are much more down-to-earth and are acquiring only that equipment which lies within their financial means and within the capabilities of the ordinary language teacher. The equipment and types of programs they are asking for and using are by and large those described extensively here by Christopher Jones and Sue Fortescue.

One of the significant omissions from the book concerns the use of concordances in language teaching. In 1987 it could still be believed that this technique for processing and analysing large bodies of text was confined to academic lexicographers using mainframe computers. In the intervening years Tim Johns of Birmingham University and many others have been demonstrating that even handheld computers are capable of producing impressive results and can have many imaginative applications in language learning. Those interested could usefully turn to the Longman resource book for teachers, *Concordances in the Classroom*, by Chris Tribble and Glyn Jones, 1990.

In the early years it was held that electronic information retrieval could go no further than getting information *about* information, since no one could contemplate employing vast armies of typists to input data into the computer. For the real thing you had to turn to the printed page. Now, since so much data originates on word processors and also with the advent of successful systems for scanning text in from paper and interpreting it with optical character reading systems, enormous amounts of information are becoming available in cheap machine-readable form. Language teachers can make inventive use of this data in the classroom and to do this they often employ 'hypertext' techniques. This is another development in software creation not anticipated in the book. Hypertext is far more than an 'electronic page turner' and it enables learners to move easily and quickly through text and graphics.

One other area pointed to by the authors, the possibilities offered by page layout and typesetting programs, has since made significant progress. The cost of desktop publishing has sunk dramatically and it is quickly becoming the required standard for the school or class newsletter.

As technophobia among language teachers recedes, and as they show themselves increasingly receptive to using technological tools, they also display a healthy disregard for claims about technology-led methodology. The evidence is that almost everywhere teachers place themselves firmly behind John Higgins' identification of the computer as pedagogical slave (*Computers in Language Learning*, Longman, 1988) rather than tyrannical master, and in this sense I am sure that they will continue to derive practical benefit from *Using Computers in the Language Classroom*.

PART 1
COMPUTERS IN USE

1

An introduction to computer-assisted language learning

1 A day in the life of a computer room

The phrase 'computer room' suggests different things to different people. To a scientist or industrialist, it may mean giant banks of machinery, high technology, the humming of tapes and white laboratory coats. To a businessman it may suggest the efficient clicking of keys, neat piles of paper and the continuous buzz of printers. For a teacher or learner of language, a computer room is (or should be) a friendly, stimulating and noisy place, the noise coming not from the computers but from groups of learners talking about the various tasks in which they are engaged.

As an example of a computer room in action, here is a description of a typical day in the life of a computer room in a private language school on the south coast of England (see Fig. 1.1). It is a fairly large room, containing five computer stations (each with three or four chairs), a software library and a variety of paper reference materials. The room is used for class lessons in the mornings (each class goes there for one lesson a week) and for student self-access in the afternoons.

Lesson 1

The teacher of the first class in the morning has decided to exploit this period to give his[1] (elementary) class some practice on prepositions. He is using a multiple-choice program, and has chosen the language items himself, using a simple procedure which took about twenty minutes of his time. The learners sit round the computers in groups of three or four, discussing – sometimes vigorously – the correct answers. The computer gives them feedback and calculates their final score. The teacher goes from group to group, sorting out problems, encouraging learners to speak in the target language, and giving them the individual attention it is often difficult to find time for in a 'normal' class lesson.

Lesson 2

The second class is more advanced, and will shortly be taking an important examination. Their chief worry is the acquisition and appropriate use of vocabulary. They have studied a passage with their teacher in class and they now see this text displayed on the computer screen for thirty seconds. It is then replaced by a series of 'blobs', each representing a letter. The

1

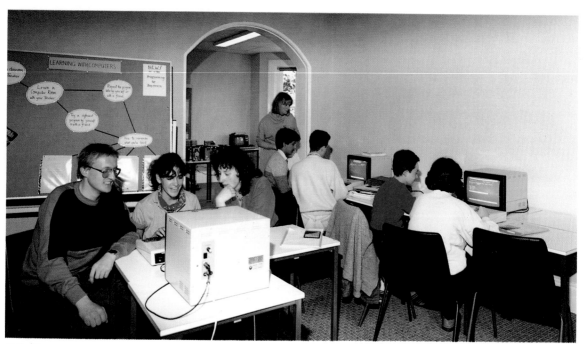

*1.1 The computer room,
Eurocentre Bournemouth.*

learners have to reconstruct the passage, partly from memory and partly from their knowledge of English, making hypotheses that will involve grammatical relations, collocations and accurate spelling. In addition, since this is a group activity, they must communicate with their fellow students in the target language, in order to agree on their strategy. As in the first lesson, the teacher was able to select an appropriate text and type it into the machine beforehand.

Lesson 3

In the third lesson, with a group of ESP students, the teacher has decided to use the computers to provide the basis for a simulation. The students are using a program called **GB Ltd** which requires them to formulate the economic policy of the country for a period of five years. They first choose which political party they wish to belong to. Then they are given relevant information such as the level of currency reserves, the amount of welfare benefits such as child benefit, old age pensions and unemployment benefit. Over the five year period, they can adjust any of these. An updated set of figures is issued yearly by the computer, so that the students can see the effects of their policies. Some groups prove to be less than successful economists, raising the level of inflation to over 1000 per cent. Others succeed in restoring the economy to an even keel and winning the general election that takes place at the end of the five year period. For homework, students are asked to write a report about their term of office.

Lesson 4

The teacher of the fourth class devotes the period to writing skills. He is using a simple word-processing program which enables students to correct mistakes, make changes in their text and receive a printed copy of their work at the end of the lesson. The students sit round the keyboard in small groups. They have already studied in class the type of language they will need, and have thought about the task for homework. They discuss strategies, spellings and grammar; they make amendments, delete and insert words and phrases. The teacher goes from group to group, offering advice when it is needed. The students consult dictionaries to find appropriate words, and look back at their lesson notes to recall relevant structures and expressions. And at the end of the lesson they each take away a clear, printed copy of their work, instead of the untidy, crossed-out pages that are often the only record of a lesson on writing skills.

Self-access

For the rest of the day, the computer room will be available to students on a self-access basis. Their teachers will have recommended suitable programs: they may want to write something using a word-processing program; they may want to try their hand at a business or technical simulation; some may want to brush up their irregular verbs; those studying for examinations can work through past papers; they can play language games; and the more adventurous can even learn (in the target language) how to program the computers.

2 What is a computer?

There are three main types of computer, usually referred to (in descending order of size) as mainframe, mini- and microcomputers. In this book we shall limit ourselves to talking about microcomputers, which we shall refer to simply as computers, for the sake of brevity.

A computer system (see Fig. 1.2) has three main components: the computer itself, a screen and a device for storing computer programs.

The computer contains the microchips and circuitry that make up the 'brain' and 'memory' of the system, and has a typewriter-style keyboard. The keyboard is used to pass instructions to the computer.

1.2 *An Acorn BBC computer station.*

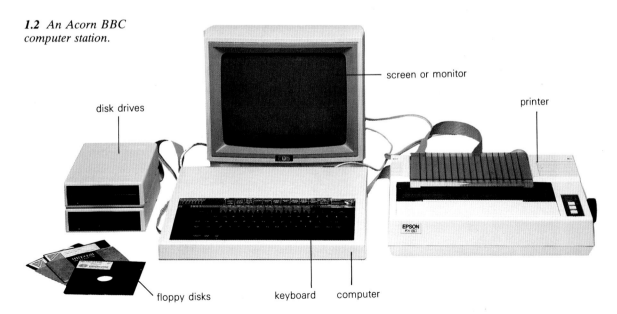

disk drives

screen or monitor

printer

floppy disks

keyboard

computer

3

The memory capacity of the computer is measured in kilobytes (or K): a computer with a capacity of 32K can hold over 32,000 characters (letters and numbers) in its memory.

The screen displays information to the user. The display on the screen may be words, pictures or a mixture of both. An ordinary television can be used for this purpose, but a monitor designed specifically for use with computers is usually more satisfactory.

The cheapest kind of *storage device* is an ordinary audio cassette used with a normal cassette recorder, but this is a slow and unreliable method which is often impracticable for classroom use. Much more satisfactory is a 'floppy disk' used with a disk drive. A large number of programs can be stored on one disk, each program being loaded in a matter of seconds.

In some computer systems, two or more of the components are joined together to form one unit. In others, the three parts are physically separate, and joined by leads.

An optional but very useful fourth component is a *printer*, which is used to print information onto paper instead of onto the screen. A printer is essential when using the computer as a word-processor.

3 Computer programs

The components described above are collectively known as 'hardware', and together they are capable of running computer programs, or 'software'. A computer program is simply a list of instructions which the computer obeys one after another, and very fast.

Programs suitable for use in language learning are now available from a variety of sources, which are listed in Chapter 16 and in the software directory on page 140. They are sold on cassette or disk, together with documentation which contains operating instructions and, with luck, suggestions for use in class.

Among the most useful programs on the market are 'authoring programs'. These enable teachers to enter their own texts, vocabulary lists and test items into program frameworks, and make it possible to link computer activities with current classroom work. Lessons 1 and 2 above made use of authoring programs.

Non-authoring programs, sometimes known as 'dedicated' programs, also have a place in the language classroom. An example is the simulation used in Lesson 3 above. Dedicated programs have often been designed for purposes other than language teaching, and thus help to bring the outside world into the classroom.

One of the most serious problems concerning computer software is that of compatibility. A program written for one type of computer will almost certainly not work on a different type. The problem is not, however, insurmountable, as publishers will usually produce several versions of a program for different makes of computers. In addition, computer manufacturers in several countries are collaborating in efforts to produce standard computer languages, which will enable programs to work on a variety of different machines. In the meantime, it is important to make sure that relevant software is available and that it will work on the computer you intend to buy.

4 Computer-assisted language learning

It is still common to find computer-assisted language learning (or CALL) described as a means of 'presenting, reinforcing and testing' particular language items: the learner is presented with a rule plus examples, and then answers a series of questions which test his knowledge of the rule, the computer giving appropriate feedback and awarding a mark, which may be stored for later inspection by the teacher.

This traditional picture of CALL is unfortunate, and misleading in several important respects:

- It implies the substitution of computer for teacher – in other words a wholly self-access use for the machine.
- It suggests that a CALL lesson is determined solely by the interaction between learner and computer, and thus neglects vital methodological considerations in which the teacher plays a key role.
- By limiting the computer's role to that of 'quizmaster', it ignores other equally valid roles for the machine – roles which are very relevant to today's communicative classroom.
- It suggests that there is a single 'computer method', and one that is inextricably linked in many teachers' minds to the days of audio-lingualism and pattern practice. The emphasis on formal correctness has caused many to reject (wrongly, in our view) the computer's role as quizmaster altogether.
- It implies a one-to-one ratio between learner and machine, which is usually neither practical nor particularly desirable.
- It implies that computers can be made omniscient, which they cannot.

By contrast, we shall present the computer as a flexible classroom *aid*, which can be used by teachers and learners, in and out of class, in a variety of ways and for a variety of purposes. Work with the computer (as any other teaching aid) needs to be linked with ordinary classroom work, and CALL lessons (like any other lesson) need to be planned carefully. Classroom methodology is much neglected in writings about CALL, and we have therefore endeavoured to set the CALL materials in the coming chapters firmly within a classroom context, and to suggest how they can be used. This will only rarely involve individual work at the keyboard: in practice, it is usually more productive (and cheaper) to have several learners per machine, or even one computer for the whole class. And we shall attach as much importance to what learners say to each other while using the computer as to their interaction with the machine itself.

5 Roles for the computer

In general, we can distinguish three broad roles for the computer in language learning: the computer as knower-of-the-right-answer, the computer as workhorse, and the computer as stimulus.

The computer as knower-of-the-right-answer

Within this category comes the computer's traditional role of *quizmaster*, which we have already mentioned. Question-and-answer programs usually deal with grammar, vocabulary, reading comprehension and listening comprehension. Recently the computer as quizmaster has come under

5

attack as a poor attempt to imitate the teacher. As we shall see, however, this is by no means necessarily the case.

Another kind of program uses the computer as a kind of *discovery device*. Vocabulary items have to be guessed using various techniques, or the computer may delete sections of a text and ask the learner to restore the missing words. Many programs of this type have a game-like element, which allows learners to compete against each other, against their own 'previous best score', or against the computer.

The computer as workhorse

This category includes a number of roles that derive from the computer's use in business and commerce.

One such role is the computer as *writing machine*. A word-processing program transforms the computer into a sophisticated and flexible writing aid, that can do much to improve learners' writing skills – and their attitude towards writing.

Another is the use of the computer as *informant*, a role that takes advantage of the computer's ability to store large amounts of information on disks. Using 'database' programs, learners can access information of any suitable kind: vocabulary, grammar, information about a writing or discussion topic, up-to-date travel information for a travel agent role-play, and so on.

Database programs can also be used to store data written by learners themselves – personal information, horoscopes, local entertainment information, lexis.

Other business-orientated programs, such as accountancy packages, are of particular use to ESP students.

The computer as stimulus

Into this category come programs whose purpose is to provide learners with something to talk about (in discussion, simulation or role-play) and to write about. Two kinds of program especially useful for this purpose are *simulations* and *adventures*.

Computer roles and language skills

The lines dividing the different roles described above are not clear-cut: for example, most computer programs will stimulate some discussion among groups of learners, even if oral practice is not the main purpose of the activity.

Similarly, it is not possible to assign neatly each of the above roles to one language skill. Although the word-processor is clearly associated primarily with the skill of writing, the computer as quizmaster is by no means useful only for grammar practice. One of the great plusses of the computer is that any activity at the keyboard will tend to involve a variety of skills, and it is up to the teacher which area of language is given the most emphasis at any one time.

In the chapters that follow, therefore, although we will group together programs that seem useful for particular skills, there will be frequent cross-referencing. We hope that it will become apparent that just as a piece of paper can be useful for skills other than reading and writing, so a computer program is a flexible language-learning aid, and will often lend itself to a variety of uses.

6

6 Multilingual and monolingual groups

Many of the classroom activities described in later chapters involve small groups of learners working together and only partially supervised by the teacher. As we have already mentioned, such an arrangement will tend to generate discussion among the learners in the group, whether the activity has been designed for this purpose or not, and the opportunities thus created for oral communication can be exploited to good effect in a well organised lesson.

Getting learners to conduct their discussion in the target language is fairly easy with multilingual groups, but less so with monolingual groups, who will tend to slip back into their own language. This is a problem, but not one that is unique to CALL, and most teachers have their own methods of encouraging the use of the target language in such situations. In Chapters 9 and 10, which look at activities designed for oral practice, we will find that good classroom organisation can minimise the problem, as it can for any role-play and simulation activities. Elsewhere, it should be remembered that off-screen discussion is a bonus, and while learners should be encouraged to use the target language wherever possible, it is not the end of the world if some of their conversation lapses into the mother tongue.

7 About this book

This book is in two parts. Part 1, *Computers in use*, describes ways in which computer programs can help learners to develop different language skills, and wherever possible links CALL activity to categories of normal classroom activity. Chapters 2–5 look at grammar, vocabulary and reading skills, and Chapter 6 shows how teachers can create their own CALL materials by using authoring programs. Chapters 7 and 8 examine the computer's contribution to the development of writing skills, Chapters 9 and 10 look at oral skills, and Chapter 11 discusses listening and phonological skills. In Chapter 12, we look at the use of database programs for information storage and retrieval, and Chapter 13 describes the computer's potential as a medium for exploring language at the keyboard. The last chapter in Part 1 brings together the theoretical and pedagogical issues raised in the previous chapters, and pays particular attention to the overall role played by computers in language learning.

Part 2 is entitled *Getting started*, and deals with the practical problems of setting up CALL in a school. Chapter 15 is concerned with choosing suitable hardware, while Chapter 16 gives advice about obtaining and evaluating software. Chapter 17 looks at the organisation of these resources: setting up a computer room, organising and categorising software, and allocating responsibilities within the school. And Chapter 18 gives suggestions for training teachers and students to use computers effectively.

The concluding chapter describes various pieces of add-on equipment, and the possibilities they present for CALL both now and in the future.

Most of the programs described in the book, and a number of others, are listed in the software directory on page 140, and cross-referenced in the notes and references on page 138. There is also a list of useful addresses, a short bibliography, a glossary of the most common technical terms found in CALL, and an index.

2

The computer and grammar

Almost all activities in the language classroom can be said to involve grammar. Free discussion, simulations, reading and writing tasks bring students' grammatical abilities into play constantly. In this chapter, however, we are concerned with activities in which grammar is the main focus – limited exercises designed to practise particular areas of language. Language learning abounds in exercises of this sort: much classroom time is spent in oral exercises with a grammatical focus, and written grammar exercises with answer keys are much in vogue in self-access rooms, and in workbooks that accompany published courses.

Computers can provide a useful and motivating medium for this kind of work. They are useful in two ways:

1 Computerised versions of traditional question-and-answer and multiple-choice exercises provide feedback for the student. In class, this frees the teacher from the role of 'correct answer giver': groups of students can be working productively at the keyboard, leaving the teacher free to deal with particular problems that arise in particular groups.

   In the self-access room, the computer gives the student more sophisticated feedback than a written answer sheet: the computer will, for example, allow a second try after a wrong answer, and may provide a clue if the student has difficulty answering a question.
2 The computer makes possible a variety of exercise formats that would not be possible or practical in class or in the self-access room. An example of this sort of exercise is **Photofit**, which is described on page 17.

We will deal first with the traditional and much maligned use of the computer as quizmaster, and in Chapter 3 look at a variety of other sorts of program that give practice in grammar.

2 A grammar class using the computer

The role of the computer as a grammar practice device is best described by taking an example. The class consists of about sixteen students of intermediate level who have been working on a unit of work called *Making deductions and coming to conclusions*. The unit covers the use of *might, must* and *can't* (*He must be English. He can't have been gone very long*). It also revises the unreal conditional forms that are often used to explain deductions (*Otherwise he'd have a foreign accent. If he'd left yesterday, the room wouldn't still be warm*).

The teacher might decide to use computers midway through the unit, to give extra practice before moving on to freer oral and written activities, or might feel that some revision of the basic forms is called for a few weeks later.

He divides the class into four groups (maybe five or six, if enough machines are available), and the groups are told to work their way through three programs at their own speed: a simple matching exercise, a multiple-choice activity dealing with the modal forms, and a fill-in exercise concerned with conditionals.[1] As the coursebook the class is using has no supplementary CALL component, the teacher has written the questions and answers himself, using simple 'authoring' programs which allow him to type in his material quickly and simply – and without doing any programming.

As the class gets to work, the teacher goes from group to group giving help where necessary. At first, he finds himself just watching and giving technical assistance to students unfamiliar with the machines (*Where's the SPACE BAR? Do I have to press RETURN?*), but soon finds that he is much in demand to answer questions arising from the exercises themselves: *Why is it 'must' here and not 'might'? Why do I have to use the past tense in this 'If...' sentence? I don't think any of these choices are right...* and so on.

Program 1: Matching

One group has decided to start with the simplest exercise: the matching. The exercise is much as it would be on paper: it consists of twelve sentences, each divided into two halves and displayed in column A and column B. The sentence-halves in one column have been scrambled randomly by the computer, and the students' task is to join up the matching first and second halves to make acceptable sentences. Here's a selection:

COLUMN A

She must be in a hurry...
She can't know this area very well...
She can't have been gone for long...
She must have been on holiday...
She must be working very hard...

COLUMN B

...because she's got a suntan.
...because she's looking at a map.
...because she's looking very tired.
...because the room's still warm.
...because she's walking very fast.

The exercise gives the students five 'lives'. Using the arrow keys, they move the items in columns A and B up and down until two matching items are in the central boxes: they then confirm their choice by pressing the RETURN key. If they're wrong, a life is lost, but if they're right, the two items disappear from the columns. Thus, as they weed out the easier items, the number of choices gets smaller, allowing them to concentrate on the later, more difficult items without being distracted by earlier answers. At any time, the learners can ask to see the answers they have already found, and if really stuck they can 'cheat' up an answer, at the cost of one life. (See Fig. 2.1.)

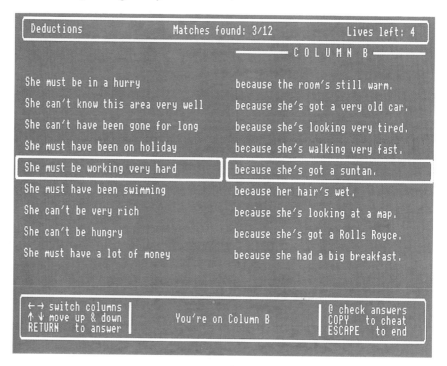

```
┌─────────────────────────────────────────────────────────────────────────┐
│ Deductions            Matches found: 3/12            Lives left: 4        │
│                                            ───────── C O L U M N  B ───────│
│                                                                           │
│ She must be in a hurry              because the room's still warm.        │
│ She can't know this area very well  because she's got a very old car.     │
│ She can't have been gone for long   because she's looking very tired.     │
│ She must have been on holiday       because she's walking very fast.      │
│┌──────────────────────────────────┐┌──────────────────────────────────┐ │
││She must be working very hard      ││because she's got a suntan.        │ │
│└──────────────────────────────────┘└──────────────────────────────────┘ │
│ She must have been swimming         because her hair's wet.               │
│ She can't be very rich              because she's looking at a map.       │
│ She can't be hungry                 because she's got a Rolls Royce.      │
│ She must have a lot of money        because she had a big breakfast.      │
│                                                                           │
│ ┌─────────────────────┐                        ┌────────────────────────┐│
│ │←→ switch columns    │                        │@ check answers         ││
│ │↑↓ move up & down    │   You're on Column B   │COPY    to cheat        ││
│ │RETURN   to answer   │                        │ESCAPE  to end          ││
│ └─────────────────────┘                        └────────────────────────┘│
└─────────────────────────────────────────────────────────────────────────┘
```

2.1 Matching deductions and reasons with Matchmaster.

The students are keen to get through the activity without losing a life. If they do lose some (or all), they may opt to repeat the exercise. Because of the computer's ability to randomise, the items will almost certainly appear in a different order the second time around.

The teacher has been sensible enough to keep the subject of each sentence the same ('She'), to ensure that the students' choices are based only on an understanding of the target items. And even in a simple activity like this, there is room for discussion: *Is she in a hurry because she's tired? Is she looking at the map because she's on holiday? Surely this sentence can be followed by either item 3 or 8? Yes, but we need item 8 to go with this other sentence...*

Program 2: Multiple-choice

A second group is working with the multiple-choice test. This consists of a number of questions like this:

The light's not on, so they ... out.
(a) can't go
(b) must have gone
(c) can't have gone
(d) must go

The students choose their answer by moving an arrow from item to item, and then pressing RETURN. If they pick (b), they get a message confirming their choice. If not, an 'error message', written in advance by the teacher, will appear on screen, and they can have another go. (See Fig. 2.2.) For this question, the error messages might read:

(a) This would mean 'they are unable to go out'
(c) This means they haven't gone out – so why aren't the lights on?
(d) This would mean 'they have to go out'

The error messages are necessarily short and to the point – they can't compete with the interactive explanation the teacher could give in person – but they serve their purpose. Provided that at least one of the group gets the message (and, we hope, uses the target language to explain it to the others) the students can learn from their wrong answer, and proceed with the exercise. The teacher is thus left free to deal with trickier problems which really do demand his presence and skill.

Used in this way, the computerised exercise can combine the best of both the teacher-led 'frontal' exercise (in which feedback is given and learners can have a second try) and the small-group exercise (in which questions can be discussed 'privately' and the teacher is only called upon when needed).

2.2 Choicemaster: a mistake generates an error message.

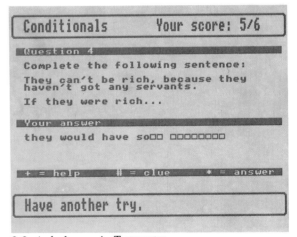

2.3 A dash map in Testmaster.

Program 3:
Fill-in

The two traditional computer activities described above are essentially 'receptive', in that they merely require learners to select from language items already given. The third exercise, the 'fill-in', is more demanding: learners have to produce appropriate language themselves and type it into the machine. The exercise practises unreal conditional forms, and consists of questions like:

1. **Complete the following sentence:**
   They haven't got any money, so they can't buy a meal.
   ...., they would be able to buy a meal.

2. Complete the following sentence:
They can't be rich, because they haven't got any servants.
If they were rich...

In writing this exercise, the teacher has had to take more care, because there is no one 'right answer'. In the first question, any of **If they had some money, If they had got some money** and **If they'd got some money** are acceptable answers, while the second allows both **they would** and **they'd**. Fortunately, the program allowed him to type more than one answer, so the students are not going to find themselves penalised for writing an acceptable sentence. Moreover, the program can cope with both capital and lower case letters, and will not worry if the typist accidentally types in a space or two too many (or leaves one out): it is concerned with the words the students write, not with their typing skills.

As it is easy for mistakes to be made when typing in a number of words, the program tries to be as helpful as possible. Both of the sample sentences involve incidental practice of the some/any distinction, and for sentence 2 many a group will answer **they would have any servants**. This is clearly wrong, but not all of it is wrong, and it would be tedious for the students to have to type in the whole sentence again. The program therefore responds by reprinting the students' answer as far as the first mistake, and providing a 'dash map' (one dash for each letter) for the rest of the sentence:

they would have – – – –   – – – – – – – –.

leaving the students only to type in **some servants**. (See Fig. 2.3.)

Both this program and the multiple-choice program keep a score. But while the multiple-choice program only allows two attempts, and then gives the answer, the fill-in program leaves it to the students to decide if they want to give up. Each wrong answer loses them one of the four points available for the question – but only until the available points go down to one, so it's always worth having another try. There is, of course, a 'cheat' key, which will display the right answer(s) – and also a 'help' key (cost: one point), which can either display a verbal clue pre-written by the teacher (**You need 'would' – and don't forget to change the 'any'**) or a dash map of the answer plus the first letters of all words (**t – – –   w – – – – h – – –   s – – –   s – – – – – – –**). And if the teacher felt it was worthwhile, he might have used the 'help page' facility in the program: that is, a screen of general information about the language area in question (in this case, information about the formation of conditional sentences) that learners can call up at any time by pressing the appropriate key.

In our class, the groups use this flexible program in different ways. One makes frequent use of the 'help' and 'cheat' features, and then repeats the exercise in an attempt to score the maximum. Another steadfastly refuses to 'cheat', and treats the exercise as a test. Yet another, unconcerned with scores but interested in the range of answers acceptable for each question, repeats the exercise several times, exploring the limits of the alternative answers the teacher has allowed for.

By the end of the fifty-minute lesson, most groups have done each activity at least once, and at a pace decided by the members. The teacher, far from being 'replaced' by the machine, as many critics of traditional CALL would have us believe, has been constantly in demand, answering questions, giving further examples, and discussing with students whether or not the range of answers he provided was in fact adequate.

Interestingly, none of the three activities is the least bit avant garde – most language teachers would probably class them as 'boring' – yet the session has been far from boring. The computer has freed the students from the mess of crossings-out, from the frustration of waiting for the teacher to be free to answer their queries, and from the tedium of having to listen to his answers to other people's questions. It has freed the teacher from much humdrum explanation and allowed him to concentrate individually on individual problems. And it has helped to transform an otherwise unremarkable lesson into an involving problem-solving session enriched by small-group discussion and co-operation.

But the lesson is not quite over. As a final word, the teacher reminds the class that the programs they have been using are available, along with other suitable programs, for self-access work, so that anyone who wants to repeat the session, or complete it if they ran out of time in class, can do so.

3 Conclusion

Many teachers, both inside and outside the CALL camp, have criticised what they call 'drill and practice' (even, unkindly, 'drill and kill') CALL as dragging language learning back to the mechanistic outlook of the fifties and sixties, and, worse still, as part of a conspiracy to replace human teachers by machines. And it is true that some large computer 'courses' written both on university mainframe computers and, later, on microcomputers, display both these tendencies. However, question-and-answer programs need not be colossal and all-embracing, and they need not be confined to soulless 'computer labs', silent except for the tapping of hundreds of keys. They can be simple in concept, easy for a novice to operate, and, most important, they can be used in a variety of ways: as self-access material used by individuals or groups, or, as we have seen, as the basis for work in class in the presence of a very busy teacher.

3

The computer and grammar: variations

Most programs that deal overtly with grammar (though not all, as we will see in Chapter 13) are of the question-and-answer type described in the last chapter. Working with a large number of such programs, especially if they simply respond with **Correct** or **No. Try again**, can, of course, become boring – as can any single exercise type.

The field of CALL abounds with programs that attempt to enliven the interaction at the keyboard by 'dressing up' the question-and-answer element in various ways. Some anthropomorphise the computer: it asks for the student's name, and slots the name into feedback comments – **That's better, Diana. Do you want to repeat this exercise, Diana?** Often the computer selects 'jokey' comments randomly from a stock, with such results as **Hey, Diana, your conditionals need a bit more work!** or even **That's what I call using the past perfect, Diana!**

Another common technique is to introduce sound and animated graphics, to make the essentially repetitive task more like a game. One could imagine, for example, a 'past tense' exercise in which the student tries to get a little man to climb to the top of a ladder. After a correct answer, the little man runs up a couple more rungs, accompanied by a little electronic tune, and success is rewarded by a further animated display as he reaches the top of the ladder. The varieties are endless.

While this can be great fun and very motivating for the newcomer, the effect soon wears off: indeed, the initial amusement can quickly turn to irritation. As one teacher put it, 'children quickly become adept at licking the sugar off the learning pill'. And so do adults.

It is true that sound, graphics and students' names can be put to good use in CALL, but care should be taken to ensure that they are given a relevant and integrated role in a program, not just used as a gimmick to make boring material more palatable. What, after all, do little men climbing ladders have to do with irregular past forms?

By way of contrast, this chapter presents some examples of programs which try to make grammar practice *intrinsically* more interesting: programs in which the 'right answer' is its own reward, and does not need to be 'sugared'. Some use graphics, but only when they have a genuine contribution to make to the exercise. Some are 'dedicated' to a particular language area, while others could have a more widespread application. All are suitable both for self-access and classroom use.

2 Some variations
Can you guess?

This simple program[1] is designed to practise yes/no questions using the present simple and the present tense of the verb 'to be'. It avoids the usual transformational approach (*The house is big. Ask about the house.*) by using a guessing game format.

The student is presented with a stylised face, which may be male or female, face-on or sideways-on, and is required to guess where he/she lives, where he/she works and finally what his/her profession is. In each of the three stages, a list of five possibilities is presented, one of which happens to be correct, and the student guesses by selecting an item from the list and asking an appropriate yes/no question. The form of the question will depend on the sex of the person and which way he/she is facing: **Does she...** or **Does he...** is appropriate for a sideways face, while **Do you...** is wanted for face-on interaction.

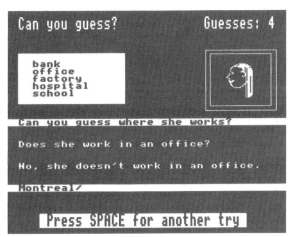

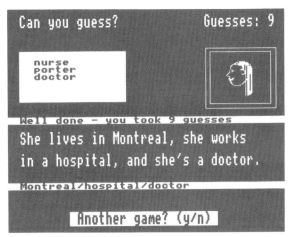

3.1 Can you guess? Halfway there...   *3.2 ...and the final screen.*

Thus in stage 1, the student asks **Does she live in...**, plus one of the five places given, in the hope of guessing the right place. The next task is **Does she work in...** (see Fig. 3.1), and finally **Is she a/an....** For each run, the computer selects the elements at random from lists of personal names, place names, workplaces and (appropriate) jobs, so the game is repeatable. It also keeps a record of the number of guesses (the best score is three guesses – a chance of just 1 in 125), and at the end 'rewards' the student with a paragraph containing the guessed information:

> **She lives in Montreal, she works in a hospital, and she's a doctor.** (See Fig. 3.2.)

The program distinguishes between correctly formed questions that happen to be wrong (**Bad luck, she doesn't work in an office**) and incorrect questions (**I'm sorry – I don't understand**), though both cost the student a 'guess'. While the program insists on the correct form, the game format injects a communicative element into the exercise, as the questions are needed to find out about the fictional person on screen. And it is interesting that wrong guesses provide as much language practice as right ones.

The randomness of the game is also significant: the 'gambling urge' has been well exploited by John Higgins and Tim Johns in many of their CALL programs.[2] And although this program does not involve betting, there is a strong temptation to try the game again, to try for the perfect three-guess score.

Finally, this format is not limited to the present simple tense. It could be adapted for a variety of tenses and other language areas – someone's holiday last summer, future plans, even offering various pieces of advice to someone with a problem.

Ask

Another approach to practising questions, and one more suitable for rather higher levels, is offered in the program **Ask**.[3] The student is presented with a text in which several central pieces of information are missing, the gaps represented by rows of full stops. The student's task is to restore the full text by asking appropriate questions. Thus in the example shown in Fig. 3.3, the computer responds to **Where did George fly to?** by filling the gap with **to Athens**. In the case of **He took..... to Corfu**, however, mechanical transformation is not good enough: the question **What did he take to Corfu?** would be more appropriate to ask about his luggage than his mode of transport, and the computer rightly refuses to answer it. To fill the gap with **a hovercraft**, the student has to come up with something like **How did he get to Corfu?** The questions can be asked in any order, and there can be a number of acceptable alternative questions for each gap. The program can act, therefore, not only as a self-testing device, but also as an exploratory medium: the task

```
           George's Holiday
Last year George went to Greece on
holiday. He flew to Athens, and then
took a .... to Corfu. He had a very good
time and loved every minute of his stay.
Everyone was very ........ and he got to
know a group of young people from
......... They spent their mornings on
......... and in the evenings they ate
in pleasant little restaurants. They
drank lots of ..... wine and usually
they stayed up very late. George wants
.................

ASK A QUESTION:

WHAT DID HE TAKE TO CORFU?

I'M AFRAID I CAN'T ANSWER THAT QUESTION

      PRESS <SPACE> TO CONTINUE
```

3.3 An inappropriate question rejected in Ask.

could be not just to fill the gaps, but to discover by trial and error the range of acceptable questions for each missing part of the text.

Reconstruction

Reconstruction[4] is another program which requires the student to restore a text, but this time by answering rather than asking questions. A short paragraph is displayed on the screen, with instructions to read it carefully, then press a key. When a key is pressed, the text disappears, and the user is presented with a series of questions about the text, in strict chronological order. The questions (and the text) can be of any kind: yes/no questions, gap-fill, complete the word, or a mixture.

When the user answers a question, the relevant piece of the text reappears, so that by the end the entire text is restored. Thus the first question – **What is Mary learning? (She's ...)** requires the answer **She's learning German**, and this restores the first part of the text, **Mary's learning German**. A number of 'help' features – including a 'dash map' of the answer, and a feature which temporarily restores the whole paragraph – ensure that the user does not get stuck. (See Fig. 3.4.) As with the previous two programs, the 'reward' for the right answer is progress towards a predetermined goal, making flashing lights and pretty tunes happily unnecessary.

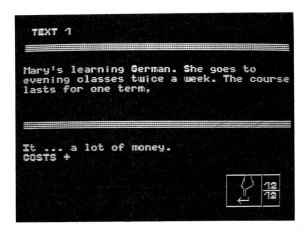

3.4 Answering a question in Reconstruction.

Photofit

Photofit[5] is one program that does use graphics to good effect while giving practice in comparative forms and the lexis of facial description. The program is supplied with details of the various parts of a face, each in three different sizes, and any random combination of which can somewhat miraculously form an acceptable and recognisable face on the screen.

The program starts by producing a randomly selected face (with or without random-sized moustache or beard), which it introduces as Bill the burglar (see Fig. 3.5). Like the text in the previous program, the face then disappears, and the student's task is to create an identical face from scratch. This is done by two kinds of command: first, a feature is selected – for example, mouth. The computer chooses a random size for the mouth and draws it. The student must then decide whether the lips are the right size. If not, he types a comparative form of the appropriate adjective (in this case, **bigger** or **smaller**), and the computer redraws as instructed. (See Fig. 3.6.)

This process continues (using a range of appropriate vocabulary which the program will display on request) until the student is satisfied that the new face matches the old. At this point, the original face appears alongside the student's creation and, with luck, the message **A perfect likeness** will appear. Otherwise, the computer will display a list of differences, in appropriate English. (See Fig. 3.7.)

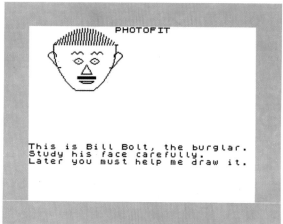

3.5 Photofit: setting the task...

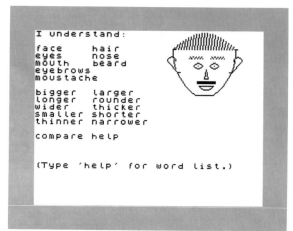

3.6 ...drawing the face...

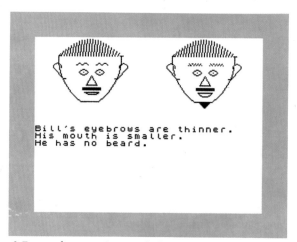

3.7 ...and comparison with the original.

With groups of students, this program can generate a lot of useful off-screen talk, and although it is limited in its range of language, it can be used more than once with the same students: Bill the burglar will look different each time the program is run.

Inverted Word Order

Our final example uses a simple animation technique to present and explain a grammatical rule before going on to a practice stage. By way of a change, this program, **Inverted Word Order**[6], is aimed at English students learning German.

The presentation begins with an explanation in English of the rule, which can be summarised as follows: German sentences normally begin with the subject followed by the verb, but if some other element is introduced at the beginning of the sentence, such as an adverbial clause or object, subject and verb are inverted so that the verb remains in second place.

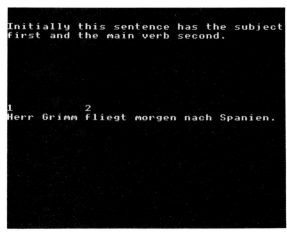

3.8 Inverted Word Order: the original sentence...   *3.9 ...the halfway stage...*

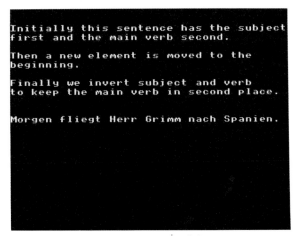

3.10 ...and the sentence in its final form.

The program then goes into a three-stage animated sequence (shown in Figs. 3.8 – 3.10) to illustrate the presentation point. Stage 1 shows a sentence (**Herr Grimm fliegt morgen nach Spanien** – Mr Grimm flies to Spain tomorrow), with subject and verb labelled 1 and 2. Then the time word (**morgen**) jumps up a line, shuffles across to the left, and ends up at the beginning of the sentence, resulting in the position shown in Fig. 3.9. And finally, **Herr Grimm** and **fliegt** swap places to produce the finished sentence (Fig. 3.10). The program then gives the learner a number of other sentences to transform in the same way, the 'reward' for each correct answer being a further animated sequence which transforms the initial sentence into its final form.

This use of the computer screen as an 'electronic blackboard' can be very useful for presenting new language, both for self-study and for whole-class use. While it is particularly suitable for presenting German word order, animation is also an effective means of presenting certain language areas in EFL, such as statement/question transformations, relative clauses, comparison and passives. In the United States, where the technique of *sentence combining* is popular, there are a number of CALL packages that use animation to show how two sentences combine into one. An exercise on defining relative clauses, for example, might deal with the combination of **My boss expects us to get to work on time** and **He is very punctual himself** into **My boss, who is very punctual himself, expects us to get to work on time.**[7]

3 Conclusion

In this necessarily small selection[8] of grammar-orientated programs, we have tried to show some of the variety that is possible within (or, in the case of **Photofit**, stepping outside) the basic question-and-answer format. Although programs of this sort represent only a small part of the overall potential of computers in language learning, they have, nevertheless, a significant contribution to make.

This is especially true of self-access. There are many learners who will respond sullenly to the class-based grammar lesson, but whose attitude is entirely different when they use a freely chosen grammar-practice computer program outside the classroom. The element of choice, along with the privacy that a computer program allows, helps to explain the popularity of the most pedestrian irregular verbs program among sophisticated and unsophisticated learners alike. And if programs are available that are interesting and challenging in their own right, then so much the better.

Another reason for the importance of self-access grammar programs is that learners are, by and large, at the mercy of their teachers, and that the teacher's view of the importance of formal grammar teaching may not match that of his or her learner. Learners who feel that their teacher is 'over-communicative' and neglectful of grammar are able to redress the balance by using the available programs. And as writers and publishers begin to explore possibilities for worthwhile grammar-practice CALL materials, so the learner will have a richer and more productive library to choose from.

4

Learning vocabulary

The teaching and learning of vocabulary is a difficult and rather neglected area. Elementary coursebooks place some emphasis on basic vocabulary sets, such as furniture, transport and kinds of building, and more advanced ESP courses are much concerned with specialist lexis for engineering, medicine and business; but for the rest, students are expected, on the whole, to 'pick up' new vocabulary from their coursebooks and readers and integrate it somehow into their general language competence.

By and large, this seems to work reasonably well, provided students are given some opportunity to manipulate and play with new items, to help assimilate them and 'make them their own'. How this is best done depends on the individual student: some take to word games, others prefer to list words in vocabulary books and learn them by heart.

The problem in many schools, however, is that time is short, and in these circumstances teachers will often make time for weighty matters like grammar and writing skills at the expense of areas like vocabulary which, the teacher reasons, can be learnt quite well at home. This tendency is perhaps reinforced by a feeling that vocabulary is somehow boring: what, some ask, can you do with a list of lexical items except learn it?

Foreign learners whose mother tongue uses a different writing system from English have added difficulties: whereas a German learner of English will probably make good use of a dictionary as an aid to vocabulary development, the Arab or Japanese student must first learn to cope with English letters and alphabetical order, both to recognise words in the first place and, subsequently, to make efficient use of dictionaries.

In this chapter, we will be looking at some ways in which the computer can help learners to master vocabulary in a foreign language.[1] Although the techniques described can be used equally well in class, we will assume a busy timetable and limit ourselves in the main to learners using a computer in a self-access room.

2 Basic problems

This first section is concerned more with word-recognition than with actual vocabulary learning, and perhaps belongs more properly in a chapter on reading. It is included here for two reasons: first, because we are dealing in general with activities at the word level, and second, because an ability to recognise words, and a knowledge of English alphabetical order, are essential before any kind of independent work on vocabulary can take place.

There is an abundance of computer programs that can help learners with the recognition and formation of upper and lower case letters in English.[2] Some simply draw large letters slowly on the screen, demonstrating the 'correct' sequence of strokes, which the learner can then imitate on paper. (See Fig. 4.1.) Others enable the learner to practise writing letters on screen: these use either *light pens*, with which the learner 'writes' directly onto the screen, or *graphics pads*, which allow him to write as if on paper, the results appearing on screen. Learners can thus ask the computer to demonstrate any letter, and then copy it themselves. Most programs of this kind are designed for use by young children learning to write in their mother tongue, but many are used in adult literacy programs, and are suitable for foreign learners. Their usefulness lies in the fact that the learner can use the programs again and again, without taking up anyone's time, and without any fear of being seen to be 'slow'.

4.1 Happy Writing: showing how to write a word.

For those familiar with individual letters, a number of programs are available that give learners practice in simple word-building. One of these, **Wordspin**, presents a word which is 'rotating' – **CHANCE** becomes **ECHANC**, then **CECHAN** and so on – and the learner's first task is to press a key to 'stop' the word in its correct state. (See Fig. 4.2.) Then randomly chosen letters are blanked out, and the learner 'bombs' the missing letters into place by pressing the right letter key. (See Fig. 4.3.) Finally the whole word is blanked out for the learner to retype.

Wordspin, then, concentrates on the individual letters in a word, but also helps learners to recognise whole 'word shapes'. Another simple but effective way of encouraging whole-word recognition is the 'flash' type of program.[3] The computer prints a single word on screen which then disappears, and the learner's task is simply to type the word. There is

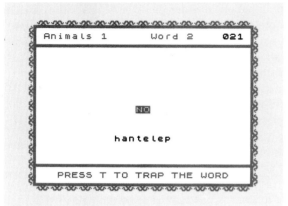

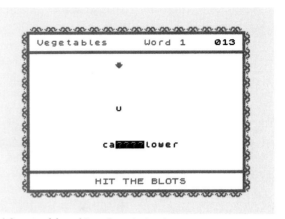

4.2 *Wordspin: trying to trap 'elephant'...*

4.3 *...and bombing the missing letters into 'cauliflower'.*

usually a choice of speeds, ranging from a couple of seconds down to a small fraction of a second, and the learner can increase the speed as he progresses in recognition skill. Mundane though this activity may appear, it seems to be useful not only for strangers to the Roman alphabet, but also to more local language learners. One of the authors was surprised to find that a simple 'flash' program she had written to help a group of Arab students was constantly being hogged by French, German and Swiss students in the same class.

Finally, we will look at alphabetical order. One useful CALL technique is an alphabetical jumbling program. The computer makes a random selection of, say, ten words from a list, puts them in a random order and displays them on screen for the learner to restore to alphabetical order. He does this by moving items around using the arrow keys on the computer keyboard. A competitive element makes the game fun to play: the computer calculates the smallest number of 'moves' necessary to solve the problem, and keeps a record of the number of moves made by the learner. At the end, items still out of place are highlighted in colour, and the learner has an opportunity to put things right. And there is always another jumbled set of words waiting if he wants another go.[4]

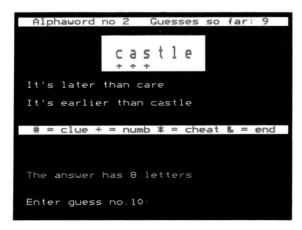

4.4 *Alphagame: narrowing down the possibilities.*

A more sophisticated alphabetical order game is **Alphagame**, which asks the learner to 'guess the word the computer is thinking of', a word chosen at random from a list stored in its memory. The learner types in whole words, and is told whether he is **too early** or **too late** in the dictionary. Using this information, he gradually homes in on the target word, while the computer keeps a record of the number of guesses he has had. To help those who are stuck, a gapped context sentence can be called up, at the cost of a few guesses. Used intelligently, this game can produce surprisingly quick results: it is not uncommon for a word to be found in ten or fewer guesses. (See Fig. 4.4.)

These techniques are simple, and (apart from **Wordspin**) do nothing that could not be done by a teacher. Their advantage, however, lies precisely in the fact that a teacher is not required: by acting as demonstrator, marker and 'gamesmaster', the computer can provide endless and varied practice which, though boring for a teacher, can be extremely motivating and useful for a learner.

3 Getting familiar with new vocabulary

One of the most publicised computer programs associated with vocabulary acquisition is **Linkword**, which teaches new lexical items by linking them with 'puns' in the mother tongue. The learner is asked, for example, to link the Greek word *skylos* (dog) with the image of a dog looking for a lost ski on a mountain (ski – loss), or the German word *braut* (bride) with the idea of someone marrying a Belgian (Brussels braut – Brussels sprout). This method of presenting vocabulary is apparently very successful, although no particular advantage seems to be gained by the use of the computer for such work, except perhaps convenience.

While the **Linkword** technique is useful for presenting new lexis, we are more concerned in this section with ways in which the computer can help learners to become more familiar with new lexis they have already met – to 'make it their own'. As all language teachers know, familiarity comes with use and practice, and a good way to practise lexis is to play word games.

But there are problems. One, as we have already indicated, is time. Another concerns individual preferences, which can differ widely when it comes to games-playing. Just as the bridge player is unlikely to enjoy Snap, so the Scrabble player will probably have little time for Hangman. And vice versa. The teacher who attempts to involve his class in a group vocabulary game is likely either to bore or confuse a percentage of his students.

In this situation, self-access use of the computer has three advantages. First, the computer is good at managing word games. Second, there is a wide enough variety of games to satisfy all tastes and abilities. And third, different games can use the same sets of words. As a result, the learner is able to achieve the same result – greater familiarity with and confidence about a particular set of lexis – with whichever activity suits him best.

In the previous section, we looked at two different programs which had particular pedagogical aims: **Flash** for whole-word recognition, and

Alphagame for familiarisation with alphabetical order. The programs described below, however, have no such particular aims. They simply use the motivation of a game format to help learners make new lexis their own. **Flash** and **Alphagame**, stripped of the aims given them above, would be equally suitable for the purpose, though they would doubtless appeal to different types of learner.

Hangman: an on-screen version of the well-known word game. The computer replaces the letters of a word with dashes, and the player reconstructs the word by guessing letters. A life is lost for each wrong guess. The version illustrated (**Skullman**) also 'dashes out' a gapped sentence, in which the guessed letters are also restored, thus providing a gradually emerging context for the target word. (See Fig. 4.5.)

Anagrams: the computer produces a random anagram of the target word for the player to solve. The anagram could be embedded in a context sentence, or alone, in which case the player may be able to call up a context sentence as a clue.

Snap:[5] an animated matching exercise, which deals with pairs of items, such as opposites, synonyms, translation pairs. The two words or phrases on the screen change randomly, and the player has to press a key when items match. Various speeds are available. (See Fig. 4.6.)

Mindword: strictly for intellectuals, this word-based Mastermind-style game. Players are invited to guess the word the computer is thinking of. The computer gives two kinds of feedback: a **$** for each correct letter in the wrong position, and a **£** for each letter in the right position. A sentence can be called up as a clue. (See Fig. 4.7.)

Noughts and crosses:[6] one of a number of 'hurdle' games. Players play against each other or against the machine. Before getting to enter a **O** or **X**, a player must correctly answer a question – in this case, a vocabulary question, although the technique can be used for other purposes too.

Crossword: somewhat dependent on the teacher's willingness and ability to create puzzles with relevant vocabulary, this offers two players a chance to solve a crossword on screen competitively. Players select clues in turn, and a score is kept. Wrong answers are rejected by the program, and go to the other side for a bonus chance. (See Fig. 4.8.) Some crossword programs create their own puzzles from a raw list of words, leaving the teacher only to add the clues, but the results are not always satisfactory.

Wordsquares: the computer uses a list of vocabulary items to create a 'letter-square', in which the words are hidden amidst other randomly chosen letters: they might be up, down, across, backwards, or diagonal. The player has to extract the words from the square.

This is only a small selection from the vast number of computer word games that are on the market. Equipped with a range of such programs for self-access, a school should be able to offer learners at least one enjoyable way of playing with, and thus becoming familiar with, new vocabulary.

4.5 Skullman: the context sentence takes shape.

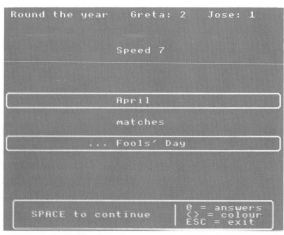

4.6 Snap: competing to catch the match.

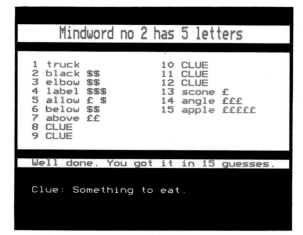

4.7 Mindword: the clue cost five guesses.

4.8 Competitive solving with Crossword Challenge.

4 Creating a 'living dictionary'

It is useful for learners to keep vocabulary notebooks in which they can write new words plus meaning (in the L1 or L2) and perhaps a sentence or two of context. This is commonly done by ESP students and students reading set books, and is a habit worth encouraging in general language courses. The notebooks can be used for revision, self-testing, and as the basis for further dictionary work.

Unfortunately, it is not easy to keep a vocabulary book in good shape. Accessing individual words can be difficult, as the entries will tend to be in chronological rather than alphabetical order (even if different pages are allocated to different letters), and parts of the book will quickly become obsolete as words pass into the learner's long-term memory. And for the same reasons that students' writing in general is usually messy – a problem we will discuss further in Chapter 7 – a notebook will probably be full of crossings-out.

One way of avoiding these problems is to use *vocabulary cards*, which are arranged in alphabetical order in a box, and which can be added or taken away as necessary. Another possibility is to use a simple *database* program on the microcomputer. Databases are programs that allow you to build up, store and access information on a computer disk, and are looked at in detail in Chapter 12. For the moment, we will look at a simple do-it-yourself dictionary program for language learners called **Wordstore**.

Using **Wordstore**, a student can write up to 1000 entries on a single disk, an entry consisting of a keyword or phrase, a definition and a context sentence. An entry might look like this:

> **dictionary**
> **A book which lists words and their meanings.**
> **If you don't know the word, look it up in a dictionary.**

The student follows simple instructions on screen to write his entry, which is then saved onto the disk. The keyword is automatically placed in its correct alphabetical position. To look up a word, he simply scans an alphabetical list on screen, moving up and down with the arrow keys (or moving directly to the 'b's, say, by pressing 'B'), and then presses RETURN to see his entry. (See Figs. 12.1 and 12.2 on p. 86.)

As well as writing and looking up, the student can delete entries he no longer needs (thus making room for new ones), correct and embellish previously written entries, and print the 'dictionary' (or parts of it) onto paper. Finally, there is a 'test yourself' option: a randomly chosen definition is displayed, and the student is asked to type the keyword (the 'help' function being the context sentence with the keyword 'dashed' out). (See Fig. 4.9.)

The on-screen dictionary has a number of advantages over a paper notebook: it stores items in alphabetical order, items can be edited and deleted with no crossings-out, and the test option gives it an interactional dimension entirely lacking on paper.

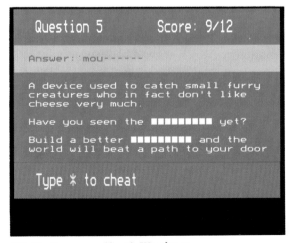

4.9 Testing yourself with Wordstore.

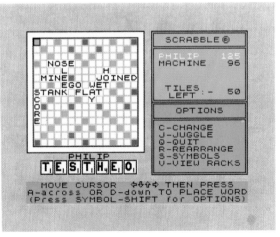

4.10 Playing Scrabble against the computer.

Such a program has other potential uses, too. It can be the focus for a group writing activity, in which the task is the creation of definitions and context sentences. Or it can be filled in advance by the teacher, and made available as a reference-only disk containing all the new vocabulary in the class coursebook, or specialist lists of business or scientific lexis.

5 Word study

In the last two sections, we looked at ways in which the computer can help students learn vocabulary they meet as they go through a course. This final section deals with a more abstract area, which we have called 'word study': specifically, the discovery of new words by exploration (e.g. in dictionaries), insight into the way words are built, and an awareness of word classes and categories.

This is much less serious and academic than it sounds, and using game and problem-solving techniques, the computer can do much not only to help develop these skills, but also to foster an interest in words for their own sake.

Discovering new words

We will take as examples of this category two more traditional games transferred to the screen, and which are best exploited if paper dictionaries are available. The first, **Word Hunt**, asks you to make as many words as you can from the letters of one long word. At an intermediate level or above, for example, **anecdote** might generate **dot, can, dean, cane, caned, tone, toned, note, noted, dote, deacon, coat, coated, neat, eat, ate, eaten, tea, once, nod, don, toe, end, ocean, canoe, cod, cot, denote, donate, octane,** and doubtless many more.

The computer plays quizmaster and keeps the score. In theory, at least, it knows all the possibilities, but in practice learners derive great pleasure in finding words it hasn't thought of (an interesting and useful reason for consulting a dictionary, this). Programs like **Word Hunt** are much in demand in self-access rooms, and, we believe, are more effective in developing learners' vocabulary, and their interest in words, than the rather trivial-seeming format of the programs might at first suggest.

The second program in this category is computer **Scrabble**, which has a built-in vocabulary of some 11000 words. (See Fig. 4.10.) Scrabble is particularly effective as a computer game for three reasons: first, a single player can play against the computer (which plays a surprisingly good game); second, it alerts you when you use a word not in its list, but allows you to overrule it if you insist (for example, after checking in the dictionary); and third, the computer being deaf, it presents an opportunity not usually available when playing Scrabble: that of discussing aloud with partners the best course of action without giving yourself away to your opponent.

Word-building

A knowledge of the principles of word-building, especially prefixes and suffixes, is useful for any student, and in particular for those taking the FCE examination. While straight question-and-answer programs are useful as direct exam preparation, there are several word-building programs available that allow learners to explore possible combinations of, say, prefixes and stems. The learner is presented with a list of part-words, and has to type in combinations that he thinks make words, sometimes within a time limit. One or two such programs allow you to make the words out of the word-parts displayed by shunting them around the screen. Like **Word Hunt**, word-building programs encourage learners to try out hypotheses and make good use of dictionaries.

Classification

Programs in this category typically use groups of words under different headings, and ask students to place individual items in the appropriate category. **Helter Skelter**[7] is a good example. The student chooses up to four categories (flowers, trees, birds and insects, say, or verbs, adjectives, nouns and adverbs), which are allotted numbers from one to four. The program starts with four empty 'jars' in the four corners of the screen, and a word-generating 'machine' churns out random words one by one in the centre. The player has a short time in which to decide which category the word belongs to and press the appropriate key – in which case, the word trundles across the screen, and settles in the appropriate jar. (See Fig. 4.11.)

As a final example, Heinemann's **Dudley Programs**[8] take an interesting thesaurus-like approach to word-classification. Each package contains simulations about a topic such as housing or travel, and features a vocabulary program which lists the relevant lexis in categories. As in a thesaurus, many words are common to several categories, and the learner can browse amongst the lists, crossing from one to another via the various 'bridging' words. (See Fig. 4.12.)

This is again a necessarily limited selection of programs, which, we believe, have one thing in common: they encourage learners to think about words in the abstract, to explore them, and to experiment with them.

6 Conclusion

When demonstrating vocabulary-related programs to teachers, whether guessing games, do-it-yourself dictionaries or word-building activities, we have often been asked 'But why use a computer? Can't you do this just as well without?' This question raises some interesting questions of its own, the most striking of which is the underlying assumption that we should avoid using computers if we can possibly help it. What would we answer if a teacher asked 'But why use a cassette recorder? Surely the teacher could just read the passage aloud?' A reasonable response might be 'Yes, but I often read things aloud, and it makes a nice change for my students to hear a different voice, and to use a different medium. Besides, this particular recording is very good, and is better than I could make it sound.'

Both of these points are relevant to the computer. It does make a change – and all teachers know that changes are motivating – to do something familiar in an unfamiliar way. And in all the activities we have looked at in this chapter, the computer has something to offer, just as the cassette recorder has. This is not to say that the computerised activity is always and in all respects superior to the same activity not computerised.

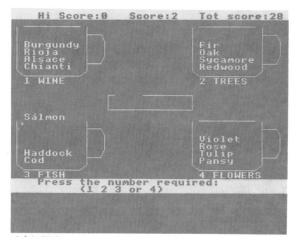

Burgundy
Rioja
Alsace
Chianti

1 WINE

Fir
Oak
Sycamore
Redwood

2 TREES

Sálmon

Haddock
Cod

3 FISH

Violet
Rose
Tulip
Pansy

4 FLOWERS

Press the number required:
(1 2 3 or 4)

4.11 Helter Skelter: filling the jars.

House

```
<      Detached, Bungalow
< >   Semi-detached, Villa
< >   Terraced, Mansion, Hall
<      Residence, Manor, Lodge
< >   Cottage, Prefab, Shack
< >   Castle, Chalet, Palace
< >   Dwelling-house, Home
<      Ranch-house, Seat
```

4.12 Home: exploring the lexis of housing.

Clearly this is not the case, nor would we wish it to be. But the computerised activity is *different* from the non-computer version, just as a cassette recording is different from the teacher reading aloud. Both have their advantages, and both have their place.

In the case of vocabulary development, the computer's advantage lies in its clarity and attractiveness of presentation, its games-manager role, its availability at all hours, and its flexibility in catering for the preferences of different users. Together, these amount to a powerful motivating force.

5

The computer and reading

1 Introduction

There are three main ways in which computers are useful in helping language learners develop reading skills.

1. *Incidental reading.* Almost all CALL programs, whether orientated towards reading or not, involve the learner in reading text for a real purpose: the successful completion of the activity.

2. *Reading comprehension.* Traditional question-and-answer CALL programs can be used for reading comprehension as well as grammar and vocabulary development.

3. *Text manipulation.* There are a number of ways in which computers can manipulate continuous text which involve the learner in close study of the content and structure of text.

In the next three sections we will exemplify each of these points in turn, paying particular attention to the third, as this opens up some possibilities which are not really practical without a computer.

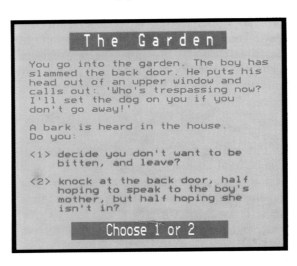

5.1 Reading maze: a page from The Garden.

2 The incidental use of reading

In Chapters 9 and 10 we examine the computer as a stimulus for spoken language through the use of simulations and adventure programs. As we shall see, these programs require learners to read written information presented on screen and to make decisions based on this information. Successful reading is thus a vital part of any such activity. As an example, we will look at an activity that falls halfway between a reading activity and a simulation: a *reading maze.*

Reading mazes have been used in language learning for some time – not as computer programs, but in the book *Mazes: A Problem-Solving Reader* by Berer and Rinvolucri, and Farthing's *Business Mazes.* The learner is presented with a chunk of text which outlines a situation, and two or three possible courses of action. The learner makes a choice, and is presented with an updated situation and a further choice of options. Sometimes a particular choice will lead to a dead end – as in a real maze – and the learner's task is to find a way out of the maze.

Two disadvantages of 'paper mazes' are the need to skip through irrelevant pages (the learner is only interested in seeing the results of the choices he has made, not of all the others) and the possibility of 'cheating' – that is, going back and making another choice if things don't turn out well, or even just skipping straight to the end. The computerised maze, by contrast, presents only relevant information, and commits the learner to the choice he has made.

In our sample maze, **The Garden**,[1] learners are put in the position of a middle-aged man whose carefully tended garden is being vandalised by a group of children. The now familiar group of three or four learners study the situation, discuss what they should do and key in their choice. It is likely that they will soon come to a dead end – the hero may become dependent on tranquillisers, or find that moving house doesn't solve the problem – and they are forced to start again and take another path. (See Fig. 5.1.)

The program records the number of choices made before a successful outcome, and a number of follow-up activities are possible: to re-solve the maze in fewer moves, to tell the story of what happened, or to discover all the possible 'dead end' situations contained in the maze. However the program is used, including being solved by a lone self-access student, the key ingredient is successful comprehension of the chunk of text that describes each new situation. The fact that the reading is incidental to the main task (getting out of the maze) gives it a real communicative purpose: students are reading for necessary information, not just because they have been told to read.

3 Reading comprehension[2]

In this section, we look at a range of question-and-answer programs that can be used for reading comprehension. Combined with reading texts (either on screen or on paper), these can be used to develop a variety of reading skills in and out of class. In class, their advantages are similar to those described in Chapters 2 and 3: they give learners a measure of independence from the teacher, who is therefore free to deal with particular problems.

Questions and answers

Of primary importance are the traditional fill-in and multiple-choice programs. Like their paper counterparts, they can be used to focus attention on any area of reading: guessing the meaning of words from context, skimming and scanning skills, paragraph focus and general comprehension checking. An example of such material is OUP's **Reading for English** series, which provides a variety of comprehension activities based on texts: these include fill-in and multiple-choice, as well as the pre-reading and sentence-building exercises described below.

Pre-reading

As well as these general applications, computer programs can concentrate on particular aspects of reading. One is the use of prediction and the use of pre-reading questions to focus attention. In this example, students are about to do a variety of activities based on an intermediate text about robots. To prepare them for their first reading of the text (which will appear on screen), the first activity is a *true/false* program, which offers the learners a number of true and false statements whose truth or falsity is established in the text. At Stage 1, the learners decide which are true and which are false without seeing the text, which, for the moment, the program prevents them from seeing. The text then becomes available (on several 'screensful' of text) and the learners can switch between the questions and any screen of text, searching for relevant information. As they read, they can change their minds about any question, and this continues until the group is satisfied that their answers now reflect the information contained in the text.

The computer then gives feedback: for each question, it presents the learners' initial response, their final decision, and the right answer. Thus equipped with the main points contained in the passage, they can now go on to other activities which demand a closer scrutiny of the text.

Parts of speech

Another necessary reading skill is the ability to deduce the meaning of unknown words from context – and a prerequisite for this is the ability to decide what part of speech the word is. In English, the part of speech will often depend on the context in which the word is found. One exercise designed to develop this skill has been written as part of a reading skills package at the University of East Anglia.[3] The computer displays a short text, a random word is highlighted, and the learner has to select the part of speech from a list of choices. (See Fig. 5.2.) A similar exercise could be

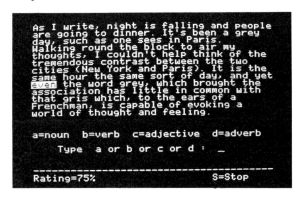

5.2 Recognise: identifying parts of speech.

33

developed highlighting nonsense words in an otherwise intelligible text, the learner then having only the context to go on. The learner could then go on to a program which combined part-of-speech identification with, say, a multiple-choice question asking for the meaning of the word.

Sentence structure

The computer's ability to randomise the order of items was mentioned in the discussion of the matching exercise in Chapter 2. It can do the same with the elements of a sentence, and, as we shall see in the next section, larger pieces of text. The program **Sentence Building**[4] takes a sentence from a continuous text and breaks it into chunks, which are then scrambled. The learner is presented with a 'contextualising' sentence (usually the preceding sentence in the text), followed by the randomly ordered chunks, which have to be restored to their original (or another equally acceptable) order. (See Fig. 5.3.)

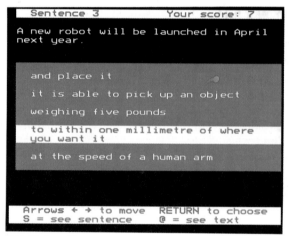

```
Sentence 3          Your score: 7

A new robot will be launched in April
next year.


   and place it

   it is able to pick up an object

   weighing five pounds

   to within one millimetre of where
   you want it

   at the speed of a human arm



Arrows ← → to move   RETURN to choose
S = see sentence     @ = see text
```

5.3 Unjumbling a sentence...

```
                A good turn

  "Hello, Jane. How are things?"
  "Oh, not so bad. What about you?"
  "Mustn't complain, I suppose. I've
  got a bit of trouble with my leg,
  though."
  "Your leg? What's wrong with it?"
  "I'm not sure. I keep getting a
  pain in my left knee."
  "But you can't walk there with a
  bad leg. Let me give you a lift."
  "Well, you ought to go, you know."
  "No I haven't. The pain only
  started this morning."
  "Yes. I'm just on my way there now,
  actually"
  "Would you? You've saved my life!"
  "Oh dear. I'm sorry to hear that.
  Have you been to the doctor?"

Arrows to choose. f0 & f1 to swap
```

5.4 ...and uniumbling a dialogue.

At any time, the learner can ask to see his sentence as a continuous piece of text (rather than separate lines), before deciding whether he wants to commit himself. Other programs break the sentence down into single words: these, however, are likely to involve several possible alternative answers and must be prepared with care.

Speed reading

One major area of reading skills development is training students to read efficiently: to avoid laboriously reading every single word, but instead to read 'chunks', and to miss out inessentials. A simple and effective way to help learners in this direction is to use a *timing* element.

Computers are an ideal medium for timed reading, as they are capable of displaying text for a limited period of time, fixed either in advance by the programmer or at the keyboard by the learner. A good example of this kind of program is **Speedread**, which allows the learner to choose a passage, and any of nine different speeds. The passage is then displayed (in screensful) for the requisite period, and the learner then has to answer multiple-choice questions.

A good feature is the option that allows the learner a chance to read the questions through before starting, thus converting a general reading activity into a purposeful scanning activity. The teacher, who is responsible for writing the text and questions to begin with, is also given a choice: he can either type the whole text followed by questions, or can intersperse text and questions as appropriate.

The learner can thus regulate the activity to suit his own ability, and there is a strong incentive to read more efficiently and thereby graduate to faster speeds. And for the nervous learner, there is the choice of speed zero – which converts the program back to a conventional, untimed reading comprehension test.

This section is not intended as a comprehensive account of the potential of the computer for developing reading comprehension skills – this potential is in any case only beginning to be realised – but it is hoped that the above glimpses give some idea of the useful role that conventional question-and-answer CALL can play.

4 Computer manipulation of reading texts

We have already seen an example of the way computers can manipulate text in the sentence-building program described above. This kind of program essentially involves the machine in mutilating a text in various ways (taking words out, inserting superfluous words, or scrambling the order of words, sentences or paragraphs) and involves the learner in restoring the text to its original form. What seems at first to be a fairly trivial use of the machine turns out to be an immensely demanding and creative activity-type, and one which has links with such well-established techniques as jigsaw reading and cloze passages. Such activities were first suggested by Tim Johns,[5] and have now become major components of the CALL element in many language schools, involving as they do not only reading skills, but also insights into grammar, vocabulary and discourse, and a good deal of incidental off-screen discussion.

Jumbling

We will begin with the familiar notion of jumbling or scrambling. Just as the computer can scramble the elements of a sentence (the words) for the learner to sort out, so it can do the same with the elements of a paragraph (the sentences) and the elements of a text (the paragraphs). Using a Jumbler program, groups of learners can develop their sense of paragraph cohesion and structure by shuffling the order of sentences until they seem to form a coherent sequence: the paragraph reorders itself on screen as the appropriate keys are pressed, and only when satisfied does the group commit itself. Then, having performed this operation on a number of connected paragraphs, they can go on to arrange the paragraphs themselves into a well-ordered text. (See Fig. 5.4.)[6]

The operation is essentially the same as a jigsaw reading activity with a text cut up on several pieces of paper, but there are important differences. First, there are no organisational difficulties or lost pieces of paper: the activity is entirely in the memory of the computer. And second, the presentation is neat and attractive: every combination appears as a well-formed text, and the screen is more accessible to a group than a desk littered with pieces of paper that are only too susceptible to draughts. The traditional advantage of the computer – that of providing learners with feedback and help – is a further factor.

Close-up

Close-up[7] is a program designed to encourage learners to make inferences from minimal information. The computer displays the titles of several short texts, selects one of the texts, prints one randomly selected word from the text on the screen, and invites the learner to guess its title. If he is lucky, he might be able to guess the title from that alone (e.g. if the word is **detective** and one of the titles is **Sherlock Holmes**). Usually, however, he will need more information: in this case he can 'buy' the word on either side (for a few points), and continue buying words until he thinks he knows the title. Once a title has been found, another takes its place, and the learner continues with new texts until he has reached the points target he has set himself. (See Fig. 5.5.)

The program need not restrict itself merely to the titles of texts. Texts could be dialogues from which an overall function or setting has to be guessed, or biographies enabling the learner to guess their subjects.

Texts with gaps

The *cloze* test (in which every nth word is deleted from a piece of continuous text and the learner is asked to supply a single appropriate word) is a well-established general test of a student's overall command of a language. Transferred to the screen, it can also be a flexible and effective teaching device.

Computerised cloze programs are of two main types: *adapted cloze*, in which the teacher specifies in advance the words to be deleted, and provides a number of alternative acceptable answers for each gap, and *generative cloze*, in which the learner chooses his own gap frequency and the computer generates the gapped text itself. The relative merits of each type of program are discussed in detail in the next chapter, *Authoring*, but for the moment, before going on to see the programs in action, we should note that the latter only allows for one right answer per gap.

An example of an adapted cloze program can be found in the FCE practice package **Screentest for FCE**. This program allows a number of different answers for each gap (if more than one is appropriate), and when an answer is found, puts the word in place, and displays the other acceptable answers as well. This last feature is much appreciated by learners going on to take FCE, as it gives them a feeling for the range of words that will fit into each gap. (See Fig. 5.6.)

Another adapted cloze program worthy of mention is **Gapkit**, which, although it allows only one answer per gap, can be used to gap out phrases and parts of words as well as whole words. The gaps are specified in advance by the teacher, who can also write a clue for each gap, which appears automatically after a wrong try. **Gapkit** is particularly useful for creating gap-fill exercises which have a specific pedagogic point, as the teacher can limit the gaps to specific types of words such as prepositions and articles, or parts of words such as prefixes, suffixes and verb endings. (See Fig. 5.7.)

With a generative cloze program such as **Clozemaster**, learners exercise more choice. After selecting a text, they decide how difficult they want the task to be – they can delete anything from every fifth word to every fifteenth. If they select seven, the computer replaces every seventh word with a numbered gap, which does not reveal the length of the missing answer. (See Fig. 5.8.) The learners are free to attempt any gap they wish, and when they discover a word, either by skill or luck, or after hitting a 'help' key which gives them part of the word, the answer replaces the gap on screen. The whole text is reconstructed in this way, gap by gap. Since the gaps are created on the spot by the machine, and not in advance by the teacher, the group can work with the same text a second or third time, each time choosing a different gap frequency.

If a number of groups are using the same text, with the same or different gap frequencies, a teacher-led follow-up session is possible, in which possible alternative answers are discussed.

Another way of using this program is as a paper-cloze producer for normal classroom work or homework. Using a printer option, the teacher can quickly take a printout of the text, with any gap frequency, and make photocopies for each learner or group of learners.

Whatever type of cloze program is used, the activity is much more than a 'test'. By being able to try out their hypotheses and gain an immediate response and a chance to try again, learners can explore a range of words which they feel are appropriate for a particular gap. They are able to argue for particular answers and defend their choices, and find out whether they are right or wrong before they have forgotten what the arguments were. As with some previous programs, an exploratory and experimental element comes into play when activities of this type are transferred to the screen.

Storyboard

Of all the programs extensively used in the language classroom, **Storyboard**[8] is probably the most flexible and the most popular among students. **Storyboard** takes the cloze principle to its logical extreme and deletes every word in a short text, leaving only the title, the punctuation, and blobs representing the letters of each missing word. Learners then adopt a *Hangman* strategy – but with words instead of letters. They 'solve' the text by guessing whole words: when correct, the word appears in place as many times as it occurs in the text, and so it goes on.

Teachers and students have used **Storyboard** in many different ways, and with all kinds of written text – parts of coursebooks, newspaper articles, songs and poems, advertisements, even students' compositions – but for our example, we will take the simplest use of the program: a group of students working at a previously unseen text from scratch.

The process is seen in Figs. 5.9–5.13. The text is entirely obliterated, and the learners can see only the title (**Superstition**), a mass of blobs, a reference to various 'help' features and an invitation to guess a word (5.9).

Having used the program before, the group know the best way to start, and draw upon their previously gained knowledge to try a number of common structure words and pronouns. Soon (5.10) they have established that the text is about an unnamed female, that there are no

5.5 *Close-up/Pinpoint: finding the title.*

5.6 *Screentest for FCE: the cloze program.*

```
That's not what I want!
It sounds like a number...

Dear William,

I haven't seen you -o- ages, so
I thought I'd write ---- all the
latest news.

I've been very busy ----- your
last visit, working -- a TV film
----- air travel.

The job has taken me -- all sorts
-- places. -- January I visited
the USA, last month we were filming
-- Tokyo, and last night I flew
back ---- Bahrain on Concorde.

-- the time the film is finished,
I'll be an expert -- air travel!
```

5.7 *Gapkit: teacher-selected gaps.*

```
                  Silas Marner
it had given him [  4  ]. Without it
he was the saddest of men. His life
was empty. The loom was [  5  ] there;
he still made cloth. But where [  7  ]
his treasure? It was no longer under
[  8  ] feet in the daytime or in his
hands at night. Even the thought of
his [ 10 ] money did not cheer him.

'What's the [ 11 ] of it?' he
wondered. "It will be [ 12 ] little
and once I had so much. [ 13 ] never
have so much again.'

In the [ 14 ] he sat alone by his
small fire. [ 15 ] head was low on
his knees. Cries [ 16 ] from him but
+ = Help    * = Cheat    RET = Give up
Enter answer 7: was_
```

5.8 *Clozemaster: student-selected gap frequency.*

men in the text (the program responded to the guess **he** with **Bad Luck**), and that it is probably some kind of story.

They then try some lexis that they associate with the title: **cat, ladder, thirteen, unlucky**, and so on, and find that this pays off well (5.11).

By this time, the group has a bit more to go on, and they are in a position almost approaching a difficult cloze text. They try a few verbs, quickly realising that the story is in the past tense, and are able to work out the 'punch line' of the story (5.12). To do this, they use the 'help' feature a few times (which allows them to cheat up individual letters), though they steadfastly refuse to avail themselves of the 'see' option, which would temporarily reveal the whole text and turn the activity into a memory test.

They can now see that the first word in the text is a proper name, and rather than waste time trying to guess this, they use the 'cheat' option, which gives it to them free, and eventually (5.13), after much trial and error, and a little more help, succeed in restoring the whole story.

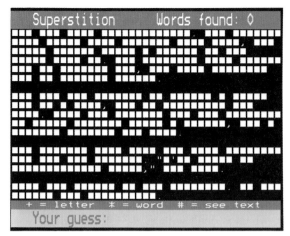

5.9 Storyboard: the text is blanked out...

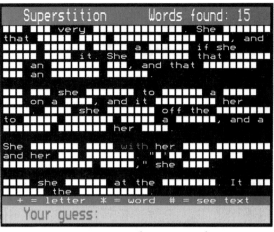

5.10 ...some structure words are guessed...

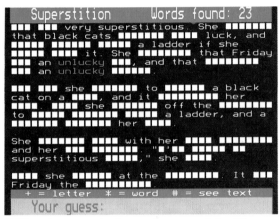

5.11 ...then some brainstorming around the title...

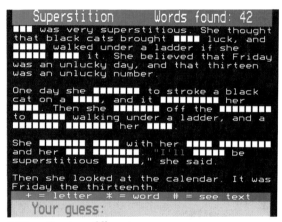

5.12 ...the story fills out...

5.13 ...and is finally completed.

During this time, the group has been working hard, and has been totally involved. The learners have had to make use of their knowledge of vocabulary, prediction skills, grammar and cohesion features. They have discussed the options, argued with each other, made suggestions and, above all, co-operated to solve the problem. The program has made them pool their language resources for a common task, and by the end they have, we hope, added to their knowledge in each of these areas, both by testing themselves to the limit and by passing knowledge to each other.[9]

This scenario is by no means the only use for **Storyboard**. Around the world, it is being used for a variety of sometimes surprising purposes, the dominant theme being translation of one kind or another – between styles, between modes and between languages. An example is **Storyboard Plus**[10], which presents students with eighteen stories on tape. Each story is a rambling oral anecdote, which is dealt with in class as listening comprehension. Later, students use **Storyboard** to recreate a concise, well-written summary of the story: they know the content, but have to discover the form. Elsewhere, a similar technique is used to train students for First Certificate summary writing: they start with a written text in class, then 'solve' a model summary at the computer. In one institution, students of Italian language and literature are given an English translation of some lines of Dante, which they take to the computer to recreate the original Italian on screen. In another, the same is done for ESP students, who work from a diagram of a piece of machinery on paper to recreate a verbal description at the keyboard. A further possibility is picture composition: learners are given a series of pictures which tell the story of the deleted text.

Further uses for the program, notably as a writing device and in conjunction with a cassette recorder, are described in Chapters 8 and 11.

5 Conclusion

We have tried to show that computers have much to offer in reading skills development: as incidental material, conventional reading exercises with the addition of a speed element, and in *generative* programs, in which the computer generates an activity from raw text. As is often the case with CALL, many of the activities described involve skills other than reading, but this is all to the good: the more reading learners have to do in order to achieve something else, and the more grammatical insight is required when reading, the more integrated these skills will become.

6

Authoring: the teacher as materials writer

1 Introduction

So far, we have concentrated most of our attention on what learners can do with computers, and on how the teacher can best use computers in class. We have also made frequent but brief mention of CALL materials organised and created by the teacher, and stressed the ease with which this can be done. It is to this aspect of CALL that we now turn. Writing CALL materials really can be easy: it does not necessarily require teachers to become computer programmers. Instead, they can make use of what are called *authoring packages*, which are designed especially for use by teachers who either have no time or no inclination to learn about the workings of computers, but who do want to be creatively involved in the materials their classes are using.[1]

This chapter describes authoring and what it involves, and should reassure those who feel nervous at the thought of being in control of a computer. Before going on to examples of authoring in practice, we will consider briefly the kinds of activity that lend themselves to authoring, and why.

2 Programs and data

As an illustration, we will take a very simple question-and-answer program called **Word Test,**[2] which presents the learner with a number of similar questions (e.g. **What is the opposite of 'young'?**), and allows only one answer per question. The test prints a question on the screen, accepts an answer, and compares it with the answer it is expecting. If they are the same, it congratulates the learner and moves on to the next. If not, it offers the learner another go.

The list of questions and expected answers is called *data*. It might be, as in our example, a series of adjectives and their opposites, but could just as well be a list of irregular verbs and their past tenses, male nouns and their female equivalents, or synonyms.

This example illustrates a distinction of fundamental importance for authoring: the distinction between *programs* and *data*. The program is the *active* element in a CALL activity: it 'does things' to the data. The data is

41

the *passive* element, which the program uses to make the CALL activity. In much the same way as a cook processes raw ingredients to create a meal, so the **Word Test** program processes its data to create an on-screen language test.

This distinction is true of many of the other programs we have looked at so far, though different programs require different sorts of data. Fig. 6.1. gives further examples of programs and the data they make use of.

The program: what does it do?	The data: what is it?
Word Test presents questions accepts answers provides feedback keeps score	questions answers
Anagrams scrambles words accepts answers judges answers gives an animated solution	single words
Storyboard blanks out text accepts guesses inserts correct guesses performs 'help' functions	a continuous text
Multiple Choice presents questions randomises the answers accepts answers provides feedback keeps score	questions correct answers distractors error messages

6.1 Authoring: some programs and their data.

This separation of program and data provides the key to authoring. To produce a new **Word Test** activity, it is not necessary to write a new **Word Test** program. All that is needed is a new set of data. And the same goes for the other programs in Fig. 6.1, and for many other kinds of CALL program.

3 An example of authoring

Authoring provides teachers with an easy and non-technical way of writing new data, and thus of creating CALL materials that are suitable in level and content for their students. The data is written by using a special *writer program* which gives the teacher simple instructions to follow. As an example, we will look at what is involved in authoring a test for the **Word Test** program. The teacher has loaded up the writer program, and is about to write a short test on opposites. This is what happens, in dialogue form:

COMPUTER :	**What do you want to call your test?**	
TEACHER :	**Opposites**	
COMPUTER :	**How many questions do you want to ask?**	
TEACHER :	**12**	
COMPUTER :	**Please enter your general question**	
TEACHER :	**What is the opposite of**	
COMPUTER :	**Enter question ending number 1**	
TEACHER :	**high**	
COMPUTER :	**Enter answer number 1**	
TEACHER :	**low**	
COMPUTER :	**Enter question ending number 2**	
TEACHER :	**expensive**	
COMPUTER :	**Enter answer number 2**	
TEACHER :	**cheap**	
COMPUTER :	**Enter question ending number 3...**	

And so on until all twelve questions have been written. After each input by the user, the computer also asks **Is this OK? (y/n)**, to which the user responds **Y**(es) or **N**(o): this allows him to change his mind, and to correct typing errors. He can also check through what he has written later, and make any further changes. When the user is happy with what he has written, the writer program stores the new data onto disk, under the name **Opposites**, ready for the students to use.

When a student comes to work with **Word Test**, a *menu* of the available sets of data is displayed, one of the options now being the new **Opposites** test.

An authoring package, therefore, has a minimum of three separate components:

1 a *writer program*, which the teacher uses to write and edit sets of data, or *data files*
2 *data files*, written by the teacher
3 a *student program*, that manipulates the data in the data files.

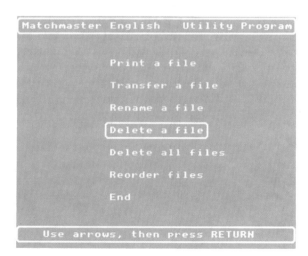

6.2 Options for the teacher: an authoring menu.

It will probably have other features, too: a way of deleting data files that are no longer needed, a printer option to make a paper copy of a data file, and a 'copy' feature which allows data files to be copied from one disk to another. (See Fig. 6.2.) Whatever the exact formulation of an authoring package, its purpose remains the same: the easy creation of data files for use by students, and the removal of any technical difficulties which would otherwise deter or confuse a teacher with little experience of computers. In computer jargon, authoring packages should be user-friendly.

4 More complex authoring

Though **Word Test** is a useful introduction to the concept of authoring, it is not a program that will give us a lot of mileage from a pedagogical point of view. A more widely applicable question-and-answer authoring program would be a good deal more complex, and would allow the teacher to write:

1 questions several lines long
2 a variety of acceptable answers to each question
3 a sentence-clue for each question
4 an explanatory comment to accompany a right answer
5 an introduction to the activity
6 a general 'help page'

and, possibly,

7 a number of predictable *wrong* answers for each question, plus 'error messages' explaining why they are wrong.

A test written with such a program would require a lot more planning and careful thought on the part of the teacher, but a user-friendly writer program would at least free him to concentrate on pedagogical rather than technical matters, and the resulting on-screen activity would be much more rewarding for the student. The extent to which the above features are used at the writing stage will depend on how the program will eventually be used. If it is destined for classwork in the teacher's presence, the need for explanation on screen will be less. With programs used for self-access, on the other hand, the more flexibility and help available to the student, the better.

This last point is particularly true of multiple-choice programs: in class, the absence of error messages can lead to fruitful discussion about why answers are right or wrong. But students working alone are entitled to brief error messages explaining where they have gone wrong. It can take a considerable effort to write the sixty error messages required by a twenty-question test with four choices, but if the test is to be used frequently this effort is very worthwhile.

5 Generative programs: the easy way

Faced with the choice of writing either a multiple-choice test plus error messages or a data file for **Anagrams**, a busy teacher is likely to choose **Anagrams**, requiring as it does only a simple list of single words.

Anagrams is simpler because it is a *generative* program, and generative programs are good news for busy teachers. A generative program, as its name suggests, takes a piece of 'raw' data and uses it to generate an on-screen activity without the need for error messages, sentence clues and the like. It does this by 'mutilating' the data in some way (usually by deleting or scrambling), and the learner's task is to restore the data to its unmutilated form. Thus in **Anagrams**, the word **house** provides the program with both the question (**Can you unscramble this word: u e h s o**) and the answer (**house**).

We have already come across several other generative programs – some 'scramblers' (e.g. **Jumbler**) and some 'deleters' (e.g. **Storyboard** and **Hangman**) – and all of these programs allow easy authoring.

As an example of generative authoring, we will look again at **Storyboard**. Unlike our previous example, which required a lot of small pieces of data, the data for **Storyboard** is just one piece of continuous text. When the user runs the **Storyboard** writer program, he is given about nineteen blank lines on screen to write his text, together with a few useful instructions, and begins to type (see Figs. 6.3–6.6). The process is much easier than typing on paper, as the user can correct mistakes as he goes along, and do a number of other things as well.

The first thing to notice is that he does not need to use a CARRIAGE RETURN at the end of a line: if a word is too long for one line, the program automatically drops it down to the beginning of the next line (**underground,** 6.3, 6.4). By using the four arrow keys on the keyboard, the user can move around his 'page' freely, and correct errors (**holiday,** 6.4, 6.5). He can also delete words (**very,** 6.4, 6.5) and insert new ones (**in the country,** 6.4, 6.5), and even move paragraphs from one part of the text to another (6.5, 6.6).

When he has finished his text (6.6), he gives it a title, and the program stores it on the disk for later use by students.

Once the teacher has mastered the basic writing techniques used by the writer program (ten minutes should be enough), a new **Storyboard** text can be written in rather less time than it would take to type on a typewriter – say, seven or eight minutes.

Writing data files for other generative programs is similarly uncomplicated. The teacher is saved both typing time (a **Storyboard** text is much shorter than a twenty-question multiple-choice data file) and thinking time (there is no need for complex explanations and messages – the program does all the thinking for you).

6 Five plus six = thirty

Generative programs enjoy another advantage over other kinds of authoring programs, in that a single data file can often be used by a number of different programs.

The Longman **Quartext**[3] package, for example, contains four programs: **Tell-Tale** (a version of **Storyboard**), **Cheat** (a competitive text-recreation game: student versus computer), **Hide and See** (a word-by-word reconstruction program) and **Hopscotch** (a cloze program). A new text written using the package's writer program can be used with any of the four programs, thus giving four activities for the price of one authoring session.

Wida Software's **Vocab**[4] package works in the same way. The writer program allows you to write data files containing lexical items plus suitable

```
  Storyboard II        Writer/Editor
Tom's friends lived in a small Sussex
village. They had a huge garden, two
horses and no television. And he was
going to stay with them for two weeks.

It was time to go. Tom said goodbye to
his landlady, picked up the suitcase
and walked slowly towards the undergrou




   RETURN = new line    > = split line
   DELETE = delete       < = join line
   COPY   = restore      * = finish
   # = overwrite/insert      Insert
```

6.3 Authoring a Storyboard text: starting off...

```
  Storyboard II        Writer/Editor
Tom's friends lived in a small Sussex
village. They had a huge garden, two
horses and no television. And he was
going to stay with them for two weeks.

It was time to go. Tom said goodbye to
his landlady, picked up the suitcase
and walked slowly towards the
underground station.

Although the suitcase was very heavy,
Tom didn't mind. He was going on
holliday. He took the tube to



   RETURN = new line    > = split line
   DELETE = delete       < = join line
   COPY   = restore      * = finish
   # = overwrite/insert      Insert
```

6.4 ...with automatic wraparound...

```
  Storyboard II        Writer/Editor
Tom's friends lived in the country, in
a small Sussex village. They had a huge
garden, two horses and no television.
And he was going to stay with them for
two weeks.

It was time to go. Tom said goodbye to
his landlady, picked up the suitcase
and walked slowly towards the
underground station.

Although the suitcase was heavy, Tom
didn't mind. He was going on holiday.

He took the tube to Victoria Station,
bought an evening paper, and sat down
to wait for his train.
   RETURN = new line    > = split line
   DELETE = delete       < = join line
   COPY   = restore      * = finish
   # = overwrite/insert      Insert
```

6.5 ...Changes are easily made...

```
  Storyboard II        Writer/Editor
It was time to go. Tom said goodbye to
his landlady, picked up the suitcase
and walked slowly towards the
underground station.

Although the suitcase was heavy, Tom
didn't mind. He was going on holiday.
His friends lived in the country, in a
small Sussex village. They had a huge
garden, two horses and no television.
And he was going to stay with them for
two weeks.

He took the tube to Victoria Station,
bought an evening paper, and sat down
to wait for his train.

It was then that he opened the paper
and read the dreadful news.
   RETURN = new line    > = split line
   DELETE = delete       < = join line
   COPY   = restore      * = finish
   # = overwrite/insert      Insert
```

6.6 ...until you are satisfied with your text.

context sentences, and once written a file can be used with any of six programs, which include a Hangman game, a word order program and anagrams.

This economical use of data explains the curious arithmetic above: five data files plus six student programs equals thirty possible on-screen activities.

7 The price of simplicity

There is, unfortunately, a price to pay for the easy life generative programs give to the author of data. And it is the learner who pays the price.

The problem concerns alternative acceptable answers. Take, for example, a learner working with an anagrams program, who is faced with the letters **SPAEEL** to unscramble. The program is expecting the answer **PLEASE** (from which it derived the anagram in the first place), and will therefore reject the answer **ELAPSE**, although this is a correct anagram.

Similarly, if a generative word order program jumbles the sentence **I went to the cinema yesterday**, this is the only answer it will recognise: the learner's perfectly acceptable **Yesterday I went to the cinema** is not acceptable to the program.

At the level of continuous text, there is much to be said for a cloze program that uses a raw text and allows learners to choose their own deletion rate: but such a program will only accept the exact word that it happens to have deleted, although there are likely to be a number of other words that would fit.

This problem is not the program's fault: it can only accept from the learner what it has been programmed to accept by the programmer and the author. The important question is: does the limitation matter?

The answer is that it depends. With word-guessing games, and text-guessing games like **Storyboard**, the learner will usually accept that the task is to 'discover what the computer's deleted' rather than to 'find any acceptable word'. In a generative program, the learner is not being 'marked wrong', but merely being told that he hasn't found the word the computer is thinking of. And provided he is aware of this, there are no serious problems, even with a cloze exercise.

There are times, however, when we want the program to be more 'intelligent' – for instance, in giving cloze practice for the First Certificate Examination. In this case, the answer is to use not a generative cloze program, but an adapted cloze program of the kind we saw in the last chapter, in which the teacher writes not only the text, but specifies where the gaps are to appear and provides a list of alternative answers for each gap.

But we can't have our cake and eat it; the authoring would take both more time and more thought; the data file would not be usable with any program other than the cloze program for which it was written; and the learner would not be able to select his own gap frequency.

8 Conclusion

Authoring is of fundamental importance to language teachers who want to be in control of CALL activities in their schools. Besides offering a quick means of building up large quantities of materials for both self-access and class work, it provides a relatively trouble-free way of creating materials which are tailor-made to the needs and interests of their own students: many of the grammar, vocabulary and reading exercises in Chapters 2–5 were written using authoring programs. In this way, the teacher was able to make the computer fit in with what was already going on in class: he was not forced to change the content of his classes to fit in with the computer.

For teachers who are familiar with computers and who are writing their own CALL materials, authoring packages can provide a short cut to materials writing which will leave more time available for original programming. For newcomers, or teachers who are less interested in writing their own programs than in making effective use of them in the classroom, authoring has a much greater importance: it frees them from dependence on commercial packages and computer experts who might or might not have any understanding of language learning.

7

Writing skills 1: the word-processor

1 Introduction

The process of writing represents the culmination of all the skills already discussed. For a student attempting a writing task, the load is immense: as well as trying to convey a message to his readers, he has to observe the rules of grammar, call to mind the relevant vocabulary items, their spelling and their collocations, and to incorporate the whole within a framework that involves correct punctuation and logical paragraphing. If he is using pen and ink, the quality of the handwriting is another factor to bear in mind, as is the number of deletions and insertions, all of which influence the appearance of the completed task and the reader's judgment of it.

Many of the programs we have looked at under the headings of Vocabulary, Grammar and Reading have an obvious relevance to the sub-skills that are needed for writing, and the teacher might well use a selection of these as preparation for a later writing task. Useful words (and their spellings) can be practised using one or more of the vocabulary programs described in Chapter 4; relevant grammar can be dealt with using question-and-answer programs, with specially authored data files; and one of the text-mutilation programs from Chapter 5 would be a motivating way of presenting students with a model text, be it a letter, description, dialogue or whatever.

Other programs which can help to develop sub-skills include punctuation testers, which ask the learner to restore missing punctuation in a passage.[1]

The main focus of this chapter, however, is on a different kind of program from those we have seen students using so far – the *word-processor* – and on how it can be used for both guided and free writing. (See Fig. 7.1.)

2 What is a word-processor?

We have already seen a teacher using a rather simple kind of word-processor – the **Storyboard** writer program, which was described in the

48

last chapter. Using this program, he was able to write a short text at the keyboard and save it onto disk. The task was made easier because the program allowed him to make changes to the text as he went along: he could correct typing errors, insert and delete words, and even change the order of sentences and paragraphs. Nor was he committed to any 'final version' of the text after it was finished: the text could always be loaded back into the program a week later, edited as necessary, and then saved onto disk in its new form.

This ability to manipulate text freely is the principle on which all word-processing programs are based. By writing text into the memory of a computer, rather than onto paper, the writer is freed from the linear constraints of pens and typewriters, and can 'play around' with his text until entirely satisfied. Only then does he ask the computer to print the text out onto paper, using an attached printer. The printing process, by the way, is quite fast: a moderately priced dot-matrix printer (which prints out each letter as a combination of dots) will print at a rate of 160 characters per second – which comes to about thirty seconds for a densely packed page.[2]

A 'real' word-processor,[3] of course, can deal with texts much longer than nineteen lines – a minimum of five or six pages of A4 paper – and is considerably more powerful than the editor program we have been looking at. (See Fig. 7.2.) As well as keeping a *word-count* (useful for summary writing), it will, for example, instantly 'find' all occurrences of a particular word, and, if asked, will automatically replace it with another word throughout. A trivial use of this *search and replace* facility would be to get the program to change the name of a character in a story from **Jane** to **Maria**.

Many word-processing programs can be used in conjunction with a *spelling checker*, which typically consists of a disk containing a list of upwards of 30,000 words. When a text is finished, the writer can run it through the spelling checker, which will draw his attention to any words not contained in the list. The system is not foolproof (**cut** misspelt as **cat** will not be picked up, although **cet** will), but in general it serves its purpose well. Most spelling checkers also allow the writer to add his own words to the list, which is useful for specialist vocabulary and proper names.

Other features of word-processors deal with the way the writer wants his text to appear on paper. These take the form of *printer commands* which can be embedded in the text. Using these commands, the writer can control the layout of his text on the page, underline or italicise selected words, and emphasise titles with heavy or large print. He can also arrange for pages to be numbered automatically as they are printed.

Enthusiasts who can afford it do not stop at simply printing out their texts. With the right telephone connections, text can be sent down the phone lines to a suitable computer in another school, another city, even another country. Such facilities are commonly used by journalists sending copy to their newspapers, and will be looked at in a different connection in Chapter 12.

7.1 *A student using a word-processing program.*

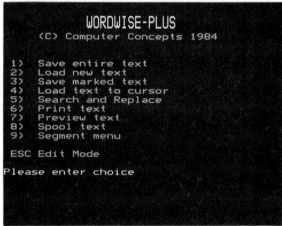

7.2 *The menu of a simple word-processor.*

3 Guided writing with a word-processor

Although word-processors are very versatile programs, they are not necessarily very complex to use. For most purposes, it will be sufficient for students to learn only the basics of word-processing: how to move around a text, delete, insert and search and replace. Saving texts onto disk and printing them onto paper can, initially at least, be done by the teacher.

A good way of giving students basic training in the use of the program, and at the same time providing useful practice in writing skills, is to use a word-processor for guided writing.[4]

In a guided writing task, students are usually given a piece of writing which they alter in some way. It might be a passage or dialogue which is incomplete: perhaps the verbs are missing, or the words of one of the speakers. It could be a complete passage which needs changing: a text about the present which the student is asked to change to the past, or a description of one person to be changed to a description of another. At a more advanced level, possibilities include a wordy and repetitive text which the student is asked to improve by pruning, an over-informal business letter which needs to be made more business-like, and a badly planned but otherwise well-written text which needs some reorganisation.

Word-processors are ideal for this sort of work. As a simple example, we will look at a group of elementary students working on a story: their task is to change the name of the hero from **Alice** to **Alec**, making any other necessary changes. The text was 'authored' in advance by the teacher, using the same word-processing program as the students are using, and stored on disk under the name **Alice**. (See Fig. 7.3.)

Once the students have loaded up the text and read it together on screen, they discuss what they need to do and how to do it. One suggests using the *search and replace* facility to change all occurrences of **Alice** into

```
Words-179    Characters free-23096 I

 Read the passage, and change Alice to
Alec, making any other changes you
think are necessary.

Alice was going to be late. She had
arranged to meet her boyfriend outside
the theatre at 7.30, and it was already
6.45.

She had a quick bath, put on a blue silk
 blouse and long blue skirt, and stopped
 to look at herself in the mirror. She
needed some make-up, she knew, but there
 was no time now. She could do that
while she was driving into town.

She ran downstairs, grabbed her handbag
from a chair, ran out of the front door,
 and got into her car. It was 7.15.
Well, he won't mind me being a few
minutes late, she thought hopefully.

Fortunately the traffic was light, and
```

7.3 Changing Alice to Alec...

```
Words-179    Characters free-23091 I
from a chair, ran out of the front door,
 and got into him car. It was 7.15.
Well, she won't mind me being a few
minutes late, he thought hopefully.

Fortunately the traffic was light, and
he had no trouble finding a parking
space. But he was still 20 minutes late.

Julie was standing on the corner,
waiting for him.

"Late again?" she said, kissing him.
"It's a good thing I arranged for us to
meet early. You can buy me a quick drink
 before the play starts."

End
```

7.4 …'Got into him car'??

Alec. So far so good. They then decide to change **she** to **he** in the same way: but wait a minute – are there any *other* women in the story? They don't want to change them into men by accident. They check the text and find that there are indeed no other females, and so make the change. They then change all the **her**s into **him**s, and browse through the text to see how things are going. (See Fig. 7.4.)

Disaster strikes as they read **He got into him car...**, and they realise that **her** is the feminine equivalent of **his** as well as **him**. What to do? One suggests working through the text and changing **him** to **his** where appropriate. Another has a better idea; use *search and replace* again, but this time *selectively*. When the selective option is chosen, instead of blindly replacing all instances of a word, the program stops at each occurrence and asks **Change this one? (y/n)**. They opt to change **him** to **his**, and this time check each occurrence carefully to see if the change is appropriate.

The next stage is to change individual items scattered throughout the text: **husband** becomes **wife**, **dress** becomes **suit**, and so on, until the students are happy with the result. The teacher is now called to check their work. Any final corrections are made, and then the teacher prints out the students' work – one copy each – and the activity is over. Alternatively, students can print out their work themselves and load up a model answer from the disk for comparison.

The procedure is similar for more advanced work. This time the text is longer – about 400 words – and needs reorganisation. The basic task involves the reordering of sentences within paragraphs and of paragraphs in relation to each other. A useful feature for this kind of work is the *move* command. Having decided that a paragraph would be better somewhere else, the students move the cursor (the flashing character that tells you where you are on the screen) to the beginning of the paragraph, and 'mark' it using a special key. Then they mark the end of the paragraph in the same way. Finally, they move the cursor to the place where they want the paragraph to go, and press the appropriate key: magically, the marked paragraph jumps to its new location.

Having got the order right, the students get down to the details. Linking words and phrases have to be changed (by simple deleting and rewriting), pronoun reference must be checked, and so on. At the end, the teacher (who has been available throughout the exercise to give any necessary help) is called, and a printout is made of the result.

As these sample lessons show, the word-processor can be used for a wide variety of guided writing activities. It is interesting to note the difference in the role played by the computer: instead of being an 'evaluator' that matches student input against pre-written 'answers', the computer is being used more as an unintelligent workhorse, an electronic scratchpad that simply displays what the student writes. What, then, is to be gained by writing on the computer instead of on paper?

The advantages seem to be threefold. First, it frees students from the mess of crossings-out and insertions that typify similar work on paper. Second, it allows students to experiment: because the program provides an instant and well-formed picture of the current state of the text, students can put in a word to 'see how it looks' in context, and if they are unhappy with what they see, it is a simple matter to change their minds and try something else. Third, the screen provides a more satisfactory focus of attention for group writing than a small piece of paper (which for some students in the group is inevitably upside down); and because all group members can become usefully involved in the discussion, fruitful co-operation is much more likely to occur.

These advantages, and others, apply equally to the use of the word-processor as a medium for free writing.

4 How many machines?   Before we go on to free writing, a few words are needed about equipment. Most schools are unlikely to have ten or more computers, each with a printer attached, lying around waiting for EFL classes to use. There is a lot, however, that can be done even if a class is limited to one machine.

There is no need for all the groups in a group writing exercise to be actually at the keyboard at the same time. While one group is word-processing, the others can be doing other things. This can be work entirely unconnected with the writing task. Alternatively, the teacher could make paper copies of the 'start-up' text available. In this case, groups could spend their time making initial notes and planning, consulting reference books, or editing on paper an interim printout from a previous session on the machine. As the class continues, groups switch around, and if the task remains unfinished when the bell goes, the texts can always be saved on disk and completed later.

If a school is lucky enough to have several computers, it is only necessary to have one printer, which can be connected up in such a way that it can be accessed by a number of machines. Failing that, students' work can easily be saved onto disk, then transferred into the machine which has the printer, and printed out.

These limited guided writing tasks can also be made available to students on a self-access basis. Provided one of the computers is equipped with a printer, the student can take a *hard copy* on paper which can either be handed to the teacher later, or compared with the model answer provided by the teacher on disk.

5 Free writing with a word-processor

Technically, the only difference between guided and free writing with a word-processor is that the learner begins with an empty page. Psychologically and linguistically, however, there is an enormous difference between merely altering something that someone else has written and producing a piece of writing from scratch. The problem is well stated by Seymour Papert in his book *Mindstorms:*

> For me, writing means making a rough draft and refining it over a considerable period of time. My image of myself as a writer includes the expectation of an "unacceptable" first draft that will develop with successive editing into presentable form. But I would not be able to afford this image if I were a third grader. The physical act of writing would be slow and laborious. I would have no secretary. For most children rewriting a text is so laborious that the first draft is the final copy, and the skill of rereading with a critical eye is never acquired.[5]

Papert is writing about young children, but there are obvious parallels with students of any age writing in a foreign language, especially if their mother tongue uses a different writing system. For many language learners, writing continuous text is indeed laborious, and the teacher is lucky to receive a 'fair copy' that is free of crossings-out and insertions. Even then, the composition is more often than not returned to the writer disfigured with red ink, and it is the truly dedicated learner who bothers even to decipher the corrections, let alone incorporate them into yet another fair copy for later rereading. Not surprisingly, extended writing tasks can turn out to be very discouraging experiences for learner and teacher alike.

With a word-processor, things can be very different. As we have already seen, the word-processor's editing facilities remove the need for complete rewriting: at all times, the learner can see an instantly updated, tidy picture of what he has written. The first and final drafts are no longer separate entities: rather, the one actually turns into the other as the learner corrects and refines his work. Like Papert, he can afford an image of himself as a 'real' writer.

But what happens when the composition is marked? We have seen that in practice, most learners regard the writing activity as finished when they hand their piece of paper to the teacher: once they have seen their mark, they are only too glad to forget all about it. The key final stage – feedback and self-correction – is missed out altogether.

Again, the word-processor has a key role to play. Say a learner has been writing a short story at the keyboard. When he has finished, he runs the text through the spelling checker (if he has one), and makes a *hard copy* of his work on paper to hand in for marking. But he also makes a *soft copy* on a floppy disk, by saving his text as a data file, as we saw the teacher doing in the last chapter. Perhaps he calls the file 'ES Story', using his initials to identify his work.

The teacher may mark the composition in the traditional way, by writing on the learner's printout, or may himself use the word-processor to insert comments in the data file itself, perhaps enclosing his remarks in square brackets, or using a different text colour. (One educational word-processor, the Milliken, has an optional disk expressly designed to allow teachers to mark learners' writing on screen.)

Whichever method is used, the marking by the teacher now becomes not the last stage in the activity, but merely an interim stage: the learner's final task is to perfect his story. Using the word-processor, he can do this very easily. He simply loads up his data file (which is stored on the disk under the name 'ES Story') and edits it as necessary – but this time he has the teacher's comments to help him find and correct his errors, comments which are no longer regarded as criticism of his work, but as the helpful guidance that they were always intended to be. The end result is a new printout: a clean, tidy and correct piece of writing in which the learner can take pride, instead of the red-daubed piece of paper which reminds him only of his failings.

6 Conclusion

This last observation points to the real value of the word-processor. As Papert and others have noted, it can help to transform children's *attitudes* towards writing. And the same is true of older language learners. Because it takes out so much of the laborious effort, and because the results are so satisfying to the eye, learners begin to enjoy writing, and that can be no bad thing.

8

Writing skills 2: the computer as stimulus

1 Introduction

There are two related difficulties facing a teacher who wants to conduct a free writing activity. The first is to overcome the difficulties inherent in writing in a foreign language, which we could call the problem of *demotivation*. The second is to involve learners in the writing task by arousing their interest and imagination – the problem of *motivation*.

In the last chapter we looked at the problem of demotivation, and suggested that the word-processor could go a long way to removing learners' reluctance to write, by easing the mechanical burden of writing. This chapter is more concerned with the second problem: motivation, or how to make learners want to write.[1]

One way we can help is to provide learners with a 'real' reason for writing, that is, a reason other than language practice, exam preparation and marking. More effort is likely to go into a piece of writing that is going to be used for something. A good (non-computerised) example of 'writing with a purpose' is the 'problem page' task, where groups write problem letters to a magazine, and the letters are then redistributed for reply, the letters plus replies being eventually returned to their authors.

The rest of this chapter will look at ways in which the computer can help to give purpose to writing tasks.

2 The student as author

Authoring, as discussed in Chapter 6, is a very purposeful activity: the teacher will have the immediate satisfaction of seeing his work used by a number of students, and this can be a rewarding and motivating experience. Here is a sample lesson in which the students obtain the same kind of satisfaction from their own writing.

The class is at elementary level, and has been working on a unit dealing with the past, including a number of irregular verb forms. The teacher divides the class into groups, and asks each group to invent and write down five quiz questions about famous people. Each question must give three pieces of information about the past life of the person, and the aim will be to guess who the person is or was. A typical question might be:

He grew up in Liverpool, he wrote and sang songs, and someone shot him in New York. Who was he? (John Lennon)

The linguistic aim is to produce well-formed questions, which will contain at least three main verbs each, and the teacher moves around helping and suggesting the use of a grammar or dictionary where appropriate. When a group has completed its five questions and checked them with the teacher, it is time to go to the keyboard.

The students use a program called **Tic-Tac-Show**, an authoring question-and-answer game which uses the format of an American quiz show. The two 'contestants' take it in turns to answer the quizmaster's questions, and, if right, they get to put a **O** or **X** into a Tic-Tac-Toe (noughts and crosses) diagram. The first to complete a line wins.

The learners do not play the game, however, but use the authoring facility to write in their five questions. Other questions are added by other groups, and soon each of the two computers in the class has fifteen or twenty questions ready for use in the game.

The final stage is for students to go to the computer that does not have their own questions and play **Tic-Tac-Show** against each other. Besides being fun, this activity involves reading comprehension of other students' work, and, most important, ensures that the writing task has a purpose: each student has created something that is giving pleasure to others. And because the questions are stored on disk, they can be used again on another occasion, or even added to the materials available for self-access work.[2]

Once the principle of student authoring is established, many other possibilities present themselves. At the sentence level, students can write context sentences to go with lexical items, which can then be used with Hangman and other vocabulary programs. More advanced groups can use a cloze or Storyboard writer program to write descriptions or narratives, and their texts can then be 'solved' by other groups. Texts in which the order of events is crucial – such as describing a process or giving instructions – can be written for use with a Jumbler program. And for more extensive writing, there are a number of programs which allow learners to author their own mazes and branching stories.[3] Care, of course, is needed. The teacher must ensure that a text is error-free before it is made available to others, as nothing infuriates a solver so much as trying in vain to discover a word which turns out in the end to have been misspelt.

A final point before leaving this section concerns our attitudes as teachers towards computer programs. Most teachers, on being shown **Tic-Tac-Show**, would probably not be impressed: it only allows one correct answer, the graphics are childish, the game is trivial, and so on. And if it is considered as a serious testing program, these criticisms are quite valid. But the value of a program depends, among other things, on how we are going to use it. When looked at as a motivating question-*writing* device, rather than as an EFL question-and-answer program, our judgment of its suitability should be very different.

3 What's going on?　　　Most people are now familiar with the Teletext services which allow us access to vast amounts of information in our own homes, either through telephone wires into our home computers, or over the airwaves into our TV sets. In Britain, the **Prestel**, **Ceefax** and **Oracle** commercial database systems allow us to call up details of TV programmes, stock market prices, weather reports, travel news and a lot more besides. (See Figs. 8.1. and 8.2.) Similar functions are served in the United States by **Dow Jones**, **Compuserve**, **The Source** and **BRS**.[4]

More local systems are also becoming quite common. Large airports and hotels (even some department stores) have computer screens near the entrance which customers can use to obtain information of different kinds. These systems are easy to use: a *menu* is displayed, giving the various choices available to you, and if you choose, say, kitchenware, up comes a page or two of information about the kitchenware department.

Simple versions of these 'information page' systems are available for most microcomputers in do-it-yourself form. Typically, they allow you to create a number of computer pages containing whatever you want, including colours and graphics; these pages can then be called up from the main menu.

At least one school has made excellent use of such a system.[5] Students use it (both as classwork and in free time) to maintain an up-to-date 'information service' about the school and the town. There are pages which describe and advertise forthcoming evening activities and school trips, lists of current films and other entertainment in town, and 'for sale' and 'wanted' pages. You can call up a 'joke of the day', and on St Valentine's Day a profusion of Valentine messages appears. If a class writes a series of horoscopes for the week, these can be added to the system for others to read, and there is no reason why stories, recipes and even school rules should be excluded.(See Figs. 8.3. and 8.4.)

The screen is set into the wall of a corridor, together with a numeric keypad, which passers-by use to call up the different pages. Although the system is also used by staff to relay information, most of the pages are created by students – and all in English. This has proved to be a very successful experiment, affording as it does an opportunity for students not only to write and design information pages on a computer, but also to 'publish' the results by adding them to the system.

The school is fortunate in having plenty of machines, so that one computer is available to run the Teletext system twenty-four hours a day. But only one computer is required, and there is no need to run it all day. New pages could be created as class writing tasks, and the system made available at lunchtimes, perhaps, or as one of the disks in a self-access room.

This use of the computer as displayer of students' work to others is not very different from our next example, which simply uses paper instead of the screen.

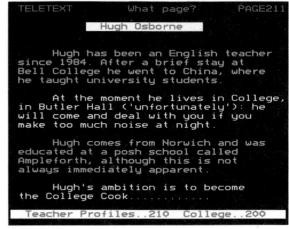

CEEFAX 151   Wed 30 Apr   17:43/55

WEATHER

Maps 152 Weather Eye 153
UK and world weather 154

TRAVEL

ROADS Key ..155
Motorways ..156   RAIL Commuter .164
London 157   Inter-city 165
South East .158   Engineering ...166
South West .159
Midlands ...160   FLIGHTS 167
Northern ...161   FERRIES 168
NI/Wales ...162
Scotland ...163   EXCHANGE 169

8.1 Typical Ceefax menu...

CEEFAX 191   Wed 30 Apr   17:55/41
2/2

RICE WITH PEAS (TAHIRI)
Method:
Wash the rice several times. Place in a
bowl. Add 2 pints of water and soak for
30 minutes. Drain.

Heat the oil. Fry the cumin seeds for a
few seconds before adding the onion.
Fry until browned, then add the peas,
rice and salt. Stir and saute gently
for 3-4 minutes until the peas and rice
are coated with oil.

Add 1 pint water and bring to boil.
Cover and cook on a low heat for 25
minutes. Leave to stand away from the
heat for 5 minutes before serving.

Ingredients follow in a moment

8.2 ...and a selected page.

TELETEXT   What page?   PAGE100

Bell College Saffron Walden

BELLTEXT: You can write a new page
            by pressing @ from any
            menu page, entering
            'BELLTEXT' and pressing
            the return key.

            Watch your spelling!

Bell Times....102   New Users..201
College Info..200
Local Info....300
Travel........400   Problems...555
Program Info..800
Students only.900

8.3 Belltext: the menu page...

TELETEXT   What page?   PAGE211

Hugh Osborne

        Hugh has been an English teacher
since 1984. After a brief stay at
Bell College he went to China, where
he taught university students.

        At the moment he lives in College,
in Butler Hall ('unfortunately'): he
will come and deal with you if you
make too much noise at night.

        Hugh comes from Norwich and was
educated at a posh school called
Ampleforth, although this is not
always immediately apparent.

        Hugh's ambition is to become
the College Cook............

Teacher Profiles..210 College..200

8.4 ...and a student-created page.

4 Publishing on the word-processor

In the last chapter, we rather quickly skipped over the word-processor's ability to pass different commands to the printer. This feature gives the word-processor yet another advantage over the typewriter, as it allows the writer to give his work a 'professional' look, with different type-sizes, italics, and emphasised print. Before going on to the relevance of this to language learners, we will take a closer look at the way this works.

A good dot matrix printer comes with a variety of character sets and printing modes. As well as the standard character size (about ten characters to the inch), there is a condensed mode (sixteen per inch), and double width (five per inch). In addition, each of these modes can be printed normally or **emphasised**, that is, made of slightly thicker lines. And if you're lucky, an *italics* version as well. Some printers also have a near letter quality (or NLQ) mode, which prints characters similar to those produced by typewriters, with nicely rounded tails. The writer can switch these modes on and off by inserting *printer commands* in his text where appropriate. The commands are simply typed in as part of the text, and appear on screen (highlighted, perhaps, by a change of colour). They do not, however, appear on the printout. Instead, the printer recognises them as commands and obeys them – perhaps by switching into italic mode, or returning from double width to normal size characters. (See Fig. 8.5a.)

```
This is ordinary dot-matrix print,

which you can underline or not.

Bold print is useful for emphasis,

as is double-strike print.

Use  double  width
for  headings.

Condensed print can save a tremendous amount of space.

And near-letter quality print makes
your final version look attractive.
```

8.5a

```
The quick brown
fox jumped over
the lazy dog.

The quick brown
fox jumped over
the lazy dog.

The quick brown
fox jumped over
the lazy dog.

The quick brown
fox jumped over
the lazy dog.
```

8.5b

The writer is able to send other commands, too, concerning the page layout. He can control the position of the text on the page by changing the size of left, right, top and bottom margins. The possibility of *justification* also helps improve the appearance of the text. Whereas typewritten text has left justification (that is, the left margin is regular, whereas the right margin is ragged), much published text has full justification – spaces are inserted in each line so that all the lines are the same length, and there are no ragged edges. Most word-processors also allow centre justification, for centring quotations or headings.

Even more professional results can be obtained with specialist typesetting packages such as **The Newsroom** and **Fleet Street Editor**, which offer users an imaginative range of type-faces and type-sizes (see Fig. 8.5b) and allow the creation of newspaper-style pages which include computer-created graphics.

The combination of a good word-processor (or typesetting package) and a good dot matrix printer, therefore, can produce a very polished and attractive page of printed text. But what has this to do with language learners? There is surely little enough time for language classes without wasting it by adding fancy touches to students' compositions. And isn't it very complicated, learning how to operate all these printer commands?

There is something in these objections. One would not, of course, want to embellish every piece of writing produced by every student, even if time were available. Nor would one want to force the whole class to learn the intricacies of 'fancy' word-processing.

Given time outside the language class, however, and the enthusiasm of a few students (and there always are a few), some very interesting possibilities emerge. An obvious scheme would be to produce a class magazine, based on the written work of the class over the last month. The actual work would only involve the teacher and the few 'editors', as the textual material would already have built up on disk over the period. They would load up the selected items into the word-processor, embed the appropriate printer commands, and print out the results. Items might be printed right across the page, or in narrower columns, like a real magazine. They could then be pasted together and photocopied for the class or, if this was too expensive, pinned on a class notice board.

The resulting magazine would, in effect, be a 'hard copy' version of the 'What's on?' Teletext display described earlier, and its raison d'etre would be much the same: learners would see their work published for others to read, and looking far better than it would in handwriting on a piece of lined paper.

Another use for this sort of production would be in small projects, or even one-off writing lessons. A tourist guide to the town, for example, would involve groups of students in writing a number of very different items – descriptions of sights, information about travel and accommodation, useful hints for the visitor, even advertisements. Once saved on disk, these could be laid out by editors, printed out and interspersed with photographs and other realia, to make an attractive four-page guide which could perhaps be made available outside the classroom.

Other topics for written projects might be nutrition, television, a school guide, alcohol and smoking, or the results of questionnaires on a variety of topics. The design and production of the questionnaires themselves could also form the basis of a useful and interesting lesson.

There is no doubt that such schemes take time and effort, particularly on the part of the teacher, but from the learner's point of view writing items that will eventually appear as part of a publication, even if there is only one copy, must be a more attractive proposition than writing a composition for the sole purpose of proving that new language has been mastered.[6]

5 Computer-created tasks

Before leaving the topic of the computer as writing stimulus, we will take a look at a rather more light-hearted application: using the computer to generate subject matter and text. By programming the computer to select items at random from various pre-stored lists of words and phrases, we can get it to 'write' intelligible chunks of English: these can include writing topics, dialogues and even poems. The simplest of these concerns writing topics. Given a list of noun phrases, participle phrases, and locations, a computer can very easily be programmed to select one of each at random and simply join them together. The result is a computer-generated situation, about which learners are asked to build a piece of writing. Example situations might be:

A weight-lifter singing in the garden
The Prime Minister having a shower in the street
A group of children playing chess in a swimming pool

A writing lesson based on this program only needs one computer, and this is only used to get the activity going. The teacher divides the class into groups of three or four learners, and gets the program to generate a 'situation' (which it does in a fraction of a second). Any group that likes the situation can have it, and new situations are generated one by one until each group has one. Group discussion and writing then follow, the learners writing a plausible story or dialogue which gives rise to the computer-generated situation they have chosen. More ambitious groups could take three or four situations, and attempt to write a scenario that includes them all.

Such 'situations' are likely to be bizarre, but will at least make sense, as they are generated from only three lists and have a definite grammatical pattern. Things get more complex, however, when the computer is asked to create longer pieces of English, such as dialogues or short paragraphs. In these cases, even the most sophisticated program will be sadly lacking in appropriateness and coherence. As with other uses of the computer, this limitation – or lack of intelligence – of the machine can be turned to advantage. If computers cannot write good sense, humans can, and we have the basis of an *editing* lesson.

A good example of this kind of program is **Dialog-Crit**[7], which 'writes' hopelessly inappropriate dialogues and then asks for the learner's help. Different groups are given different 'dialogues' to work on, or they could all be given the same one, with a vote at the end for the best group adaptation.

Perhaps the most interesting programs of this type are those which generate 'poetry'. There are several *haiku*-generating programs, which arrange randomly selected words in a vaguely grammatical grouping and with a 5-7-5 arrangement of syllables. One program, **Poetic Pam**, allows the user to decide on the number of lines, the number of beats to each line, and a rhyming scheme (for example, **ababcc** or **aabbc ddeecff**), and then prints out a 'poem' which is grammatically sound, and parts of which may make some sense. Figs. 8.6 and 8.7 show some sample outputs:[8]

White eagles gliding,
Soaring o'er the black garden:
Golden remembrance.

Troubled ghosts breathing,
Gliding through the loveless depths:
Frightened emptiness.

8.6 Two computer-generated haiku.

61

Wasting time displays your jest.
What do I give? Joy!
The sin should be green: the life might be blessed.
Should Mary my breast destroy?

A rest of rest converts my heart.
A wife of John does please.
Mary may not believe that art.
Why do you start to freeze?

Wayward soul is art and shade.
My drooling bridegroom is green.
A lover wishes a love to fade.
Work and a sin is obscene.

My friend does not delay so well.
A rhyme does not delay in hell.

8.7 A sonnet (in need of human intervention) from Poetic Pam.

Besides being fascinating in their own right, poetry-generating programs can be put to good use with higher-level language learners, especially with the recent reawakening of interest in poetry in language-learning circles. Most obvious is for students to edit a computer 'poem' into an acceptable form. Indeed, **Poetic Pam** has an editing feature built into it for just such a purpose.

A more interesting possibility is for learners to keep the program producing poems until it comes up with something that could possibly have some meaning. With short poems like *haiku*, this happens surprisingly often, and in any case poems are not necessarily expected to 'make sense' in any conventional way. The group can then discuss among themselves what the poem might mean, then 'present' it to the rest of the class as if it was a real poem by a real poet, or perhaps write an explanation of its meaning as a composition.

A final, and equally intriguing, possibility is for learners to create the lists from which the program selects its words, and perhaps devise new grammatical structures for, say, a *haiku* program. For an advanced class, the selection of items that will make sense when assembled randomly by the machine could be an enlightening and fascinating activity.

6 Conclusion

The last two chapters have concentrated on the computer as a motivating tool, both as a labour-saving device and as a 'publisher' of students' writing.

The last section was perhaps more experimental, and suggested how the computer might stimulate both writing and talking, by providing 'something to write about', and we will see more examples of this in later chapters. In the next two chapters we develop the idea of the computer as provider of subject matter, this time focussing mainly on oral skills.

9

Oral skills 1: simulations and role-plays

1 Introduction

In earlier chapters we have tried to show how computers can stimulate communication among language learners. So far this oral interaction has been a side effect, albeit a valuable one, of activities in which our main aim was to help learners develop other skills. In this chapter and the next, by contrast, we will be looking at CALL activities in which oral communication in the target language is the primary focus.

In today's language classrooms, considerable emphasis is given to free oral activities in which learners use the language they have learned to communicate with each other. These activities include simulations, role-plays and discussions. Computer *simulations* can provide a motivating stimulus for such work, as they offer both a focus for oral activity and a continually changing scenario for learners to talk about.[1]

As with any conventional classroom simulation or role-play, activities using computer simulations need careful preparation and careful management, and should not be undertaken lightly. We hope to show,

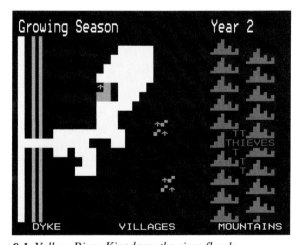

9.1 *Yellow River Kingdom: the river floods...*

9.2 *...Time to count the cost.*

however, that the extra effort can be worthwhile and that, used wisely, computers have a useful contribution to make to the development of oral skills. This is best done by taking a typical simulation program and describing how it can be integrated into a lesson or series of lessons.

2 Yellow River Kingdom

Yellow River Kingdom provides a simple simulation of life in a poor rice-growing economy. The kingdom consists of a cluster of three villages situated between a river to the west and mountains to the east. A dyke separates the river from the fields; bandits lurk in the mountains.

The ruler of the kingdom has only two natural resources at his disposal: the population itself, and a number of baskets of rice, which is used both to feed the population and to plant the fields. There are three seasons: a winter season, a growing season and a harvesting season. At the beginning of each season, the ruler must decide how many people to allocate to various tasks: that is, how many should work in the fields, how many should maintain the dyke, and how many should protect the villages against bandits. The allocation is crucial. If the dyke is undermanned, the river may overflow into the fields and the harvest may be ruined. If too few people are guarding the villages, the bandits may come down from the mountains to steal rice, killing as they go. If there are not enough people working in the fields, the harvest will suffer, and people may starve. (See Fig. 9.1.)

Each growing season, an additional decision is needed: the amount of rice to be planted in the fields. This decision will in turn affect the size of the harvest, and will also determine how much rice is left in the meantime for feeding the population.

After keying in the figures for a season, the ruler watches with horror (or relief) as the river floods (or doesn't flood) and the bandits attack (or don't attack) the villages. He is then told how many deaths, if any, there have been from flooding or attack, the current level of population, how many baskets of rice have been lost, and how many remain. Decisions must then be made for the next season. (See Fig. 9.2.)

The way things go depends partly on the ruler's decisions, partly on other factors such as the severity of the winter and the strength of the bandits (which the machine determines by generating random numbers). The combination of these two factors ensures that the results are different each time the program is used. Some rulers manage to eradicate the entire population within two years; others rule for twenty-five years or more. Some will find bandits coming down from the mountains to join the kingdom; others that all their food has been looted. The common denominator is the high level of communication that the activity stimulates if the group of students acting as ruler has been adequately prepared for the task.

3 Using the program

Exactly how **Yellow River Kingdom** is used will depend on the class size and the number of computers available. In any event, the lesson or lessons will fall into the three phases common to all language simulations: *preparation, activity* and *follow-up.*

During the preparation phase, the teacher introduces the class to the program, and takes them through two or three sample seasons. This gives an opportunity to deal with any new vocabulary items, such as *bandit, harvest* and *dyke.* Some revision of useful structures and functions is also needed, including suggestions, reason-giving, speculation and, no doubt, recrimination and regret.

The language exponents singled out for special attention will depend on whether the activity is to be a *simulation* (with learners just being themselves) or a *role-play* (in which they will take the parts of government ministers and advisers). If the former, more informal language will be appropriate, and the teacher might suggest expressions like *Maybe we should..., Don't you think we ought to..., I wonder what would happen if...*

A role-play will demand preparation in more formal language: proposing and (politely) opposing strategies; interrupting; summarising opinions; analysing facts and figures. And different characters will have to be given (or to prepare for themselves) the 'line' they will follow in cabinet meetings.

If several computers are available, the simplest way of conducting the activity is to divide the class into groups and let each group work through the program at its own speed, either as a simulation or a role-play.

The activity will, however, need to be monitored carefully by the teacher. In the context in which learners find themselves – grouped around a keyboard and asked to type in numbers – a fairly restricted range of language is sufficient to communicate their opinions and decisions: a lazy group may even limit themselves to calling out numbers, and a monolingual group may lapse into the mother tongue when they start getting involved in the game.

One way of discouraging these tendencies is to allot roles: a Prime Minister, who chairs the discussion and whose decision is final, a Minister of Agriculture (the fields), a Minister of Defence (the bandits), a Minister of Works (the river), and a Civil Servant, whose job it is to implement cabinet decisions by feeding them into the computer. If the various characters are competing for the kingdom's manpower, they will have to justify their demands, and thus give the Prime Minister something on which to base his or her decisions.

Perhaps the best way to conduct a role-play is to remove its participants from the computer altogether, by placing them at a table a few feet from the machine, or even in the next room. The temptation to use restricted 'computer-speak' is thus removed, and the Civil Servant has an extra task: to report back to cabinet the results of their decisions. This technique dramatically increases the amount and quality of language used, so much so that a group can spend as long as fifty minutes in intense discussion and argument and get through no more than five or six seasons.[2]

The technique is also ideal for small classes that have only one computer. The teacher can monitor the whole activity, interrupting if necessary. With larger classes, one possibility is for one group of learners to use the program while the others do something else. Another is to widen the discussion to include the whole class, by allotting roles to groups, each with a spokesman who relays the group's opinions to the rest of the class.

Feedback

Adequate feedback is at least as important as preparation. A feedback session gives the different groups the opportunity to tell each other and the teacher what their particular experiences were: how many years they managed to rule, the problems they encountered, and the different tactics they adopted for each season. These experiences can later be written up as homework, either as a direct description of what happened, or in the form of a newspaper article, a letter from a villager to a relative living elsewhere, or a report from a government minister to the Head of State.

The session is also an opportunity for learners to get feedback on the quality of the language used during the activity. This can come both from the teacher, who has been listening in throughout, and from the learners themselves, who should be encouraged to analyse the aspects of their linguistic performance they felt to be successful and less than successful.

4 Other simulation programs

There are a number of other computer simulations that are suitable for classroom use. In general, they run along the same lines as **Yellow River Kingdom**, in that they operate in repeated cycles, and involve the user in the management of some kind of system. Their subject matter is usually, but by no means always, some kind of economy or business venture, and this, together with the high level of realism attained by some simulations, makes them particularly suitable for learners of business English.

A good example is **GB Ltd**, which entails running not a cluster of villages but the British economy. Learners begin by choosing to which political party (Labour, Conservative, Liberal or Social Democrat) they

```
        RT HON Simon Hackett PM

      Term  :  1          Year  :  2
 Inflation :  78%  Unemployment  :  2.1M.
   Reforms :  0    Exchange Rate :  $0.61/£
  Pop.Rtng :  19   Acc.Bal :£   -71250M.

           REFORM OPPORTUNITIES

 A  Improve Health Service    :£     25M
 B  Build New Homes           :£      0M
 C  Jobs for School Leavers   :£     25M
 D  Build New Schools         :£      0M
 E  Improve Road System       :£     30M

 F  When finished

       Enter PREFIX of reform to change
 ?
```

9.3 GB Ltd: inflation getting out of hand.

```
 f1 Weather Forecast         f2 Visitors

                  Day 3
    Credit        Time        Spending
    £689.75      0:08:51      £287.75


 Tins of coffee (for 100 cups).
 Quantity? 4   @ £4.00  = £16.00

                             Cost Stock Buying
 Round rolls .........       10p     0    300
 Long rolls ..........        8p     0    350
 Hamburgers ..........       20p     0    300
 Frankfurters .......        60p     0     35
→Coffee .............    £4.00       0
 Cola ...............        15p     0    150
 Sunglasses .........        90p     0     60
 Umbrellas ..........     £2.25      5     25


 ─────────────────────────────────────────
      Use the arrow keys to select item.
```

9.4 Fast Food: buying in stock.

wish to belong. They are then given information about the country's economy, which includes the rate of inflation, the exchange rate against the dollar, currency reserves, unemployment figures and the government's popularity rating. (See Fig. 9.3.)

They then run the country for a period of five years, deciding on rates of taxation, duty on cigarettes, alcohol and petrol, unemployment and child benefits, and old age pensions. Feedback is given at the end of each year. At the end of the five year period there is a general election, the results of which indicate the popularity and effectiveness of the learners' policies.

As well as providing an ideal context in which to introduce the vocabulary of politics and economics and the concepts behind them, **GB Ltd** provokes a high level of debate among learners, and once used, is likely to be used again, both in class and for self-access.

Fast Food is one of a number of programs which simulate the day-to-day operation of a small business. This time the task is to run a refreshment stall at an exhibition for a period of a few days. Using the daily information given, which includes a weather forecast and the attendance figures for the equivalent day during last year's exhibition, learners decide how much stock to buy of various foods and drinks (from a limited budget), and how much to charge for them. (See Fig. 9.4.) The feedback stage reveals which items sold out (and at what time of day), remaining stocks, and the day's profits. If a computer network is being used, several refreshment stalls can be run in competition with each other by groups of students at different machines.

Other business simulations involve the user in running a television factory (**Telemark**), a paraffin company (**Paraffin File**) and a company producing car door alarms (**Bleeper**),[3] and several are available that simulate trading in stocks and shares (e.g. **Stokmark**). This last type has a special advantage for classes that have only one computer, in that stock market programs usually allow a number of investors to operate at the same time. (See Fig. 9.5.) Groups of learners, acting as investment

```
 Rudi, your cash is £200

 SHARES          Price   Div.   Yield  P/E

 C) Colemine  111p     10     9        5
 D) Derfoods   90p     10    11.11     4
 E) Electrix  100p     10    10        5
 F) Fintrust  110p     10     9.09     5

 HOLDINGS        (C)    (D)    (E)    (F)

 Rudi            0      0      0      1000
 Teresa          750    0      0      0
 Laura           0      0      0      900
 Kurt            600    0      0      0



 Which shares will you trade?
```

9.5 Stokmark: buying and selling shares.

```
         Matt's General Store
         Independence, Missouri

                   April 1, 1848

     1. Oxen              $120.00
     2. Food              $160.00
     3. Clothing            $0.00
     4. Ammunition         $20.00
     5. Spare parts         $0.00

         Total bill:      $300.00

     Amount you have:     $400.00

     Which item would you
     like to buy? ▓

     Press SPACE BAR to
     leave store
```

9.6 Buying supplies before embarking on the Oregon Trail.

syndicates, can therefore work in competition, discussing their strategy away from the computer, and taking it in turns to send 'runners' to the keyboard to feed in decisions and relay news back to the group.[4]

Although business-style simulations are particularly useful for ESP learners, computer simulations are by no means limited to this field of interest. At least one program, **Football Manager**, allows the learner to manage a football team for a number of seasons, while the **Sailing Ships Game** puts him in charge of a sailing ship plying its route around the world in widely different weather conditions at different times of year. And for Western fans, **The Oregon Trail** takes the user along the route used by early settlers in the United States. (See Fig. 9.6.)

Our final example is **Osprey**, which takes for its theme an ecological problem: the fast decreasing number of ospreys in Scotland. Learners have to protect the remaining birds using a team of wardens to prevent egg-stealers, hunters and tourists from disturbing the nests, the aim being to halt the decline and reestablish a healthy population of birds.

One advantage of computer simulations, therefore, is the wide variety of subject matter they deal with: because simulations written in English are widely used in educational fields other than language learning, such as geography and history, the English teacher is ensured of a rich supply of simulation programs for learners with all sorts of interests. We will now look at the pedagogical advantages.

5 Why use computer simulations?

The major advantage of computer simulations is that they are very motivating – sometimes so motivating that care is needed to keep learners from slipping back into the mother tongue. By exploiting the speed and number-crunching capacities of the computer within a framework that provokes discussions, programs like **GB Ltd** provide a basis for activities that would be impossible – or certainly much slower and less convincing – using any other medium. They give learners instant feedback on the effects of their decisions, and this feedback itself stimulates arguments and comments, suggestions and counter-suggestions.

Moreover, the feedback the computer gives (in the form of an updated situation) is authoritative: it is accepted by learners as being the results of their decisions, in a way that similar feedback coming from the teacher might not be. There is no arguing with its judgment, no going back on unwise decisions, and no 'cheating' (as was mentioned in the section on reading mazes in Chapter 5).

Because of the generally acceptable and comprehensive feedback given by the computer, the activity by and large manages itself. After the preparation stage, the teacher is therefore free to take a back seat and concentrate on the language used and the strategies adopted by the learners, in preparation for the feedback session.

The teacher may, on the other hand, want to intervene during the simulation, perhaps to deal with a language problem or give some tactical advice. With a conventional simulation or role-play, this can be a problem, and the teacher will tend to refrain from interrupting, even if the point is important, knowing that the learners will find it difficult to get going again. The interruption will destroy the illusion of reality that the teacher and learners have built up so carefully, and everybody will forget where they had got to before they stopped. The effect of interruption on a computer simulation, however, need not be so disastrous. The cyclical nature of the activity – in days, seasons or years – provides a series of natural stopping places, and, more important, there is no danger of learners 'losing their place': an up-to-date summary of the situation remains frozen on the screen during each interruption, and is ready to act as the focus of attention as soon as the action restarts.

6 Conclusion

In *Mindstorms*, Papert suggests that the best learning takes place when the learner is in charge.[5] To a large extent this is true when learners work on computer simulations. They decide what action to take, and the computer tells them the consequences of their action. Even the teacher does not know exactly how the action will develop, as this depends on the learners' decisions and the random numbers generated by the computer.

The students therefore have a reason for speaking, since they need to communicate their opinions to the other members of the group, and a context within which to speak, that is, the framework of the activity.

We would not suggest that this kind of activity should take place every week. But even if it is done only once or twice a term, it will add an extra dimension to a language course, bringing an aspect of the outside world into the classroom and providing a new context within which learners can practise the language acquired in more orthodox lessons.

10

Oral skills 2: adventures

1 What are adventures? [1]

A: GO NORTH
B: THE RATTLESNAKE WON'T LET YOU GO NORTH
A: KILL SNAKE
B: WITH WHAT?
A: THROW KNIFE
B: YOUR KNIFE IS NOT BIG ENOUGH TO KILL THIS SNAKE
A: THROW ROCK
B: YOU AREN'T CARRYING IT
A: TAKE ROCK
B: THE ROCK IS MUCH TOO BIG
A: GO NORTH
B: THE RATTLESNAKE WON'T LET YOU GO NORTH....

(See Fig. 10.1.)

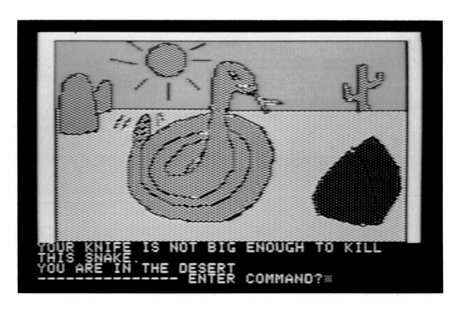

10.1 *The Wizard and the Princess: trouble with snakes.*

70

This dialogue, between human (A) and computer (B), takes place (or may take place) near the beginning of **The Wizard and the Princess**, an adventure game written for the Apple computer. An adventure game is a kind of computer simulation, but one which differs from those we looked at in the last chapter in two respects:

1   It is a single story with a definite 'plot', rather than a repeatable and cyclical scenario that turns out differently each time it is used.

2   It accepts commands typed in a kind of 'simple English', usually a verb-noun combination without articles or prepositions.

In an adventure, the computer acts as the player's eyes, ears, arms and legs, as he or she attempts to fulfil a task which is always fraught with danger, and is more often than not exotic, violent and sexist. The task in the above adventure is to rescue a princess who has been kidnapped by an evil wizard (in return for her hand and half the kingdom), and involves the adventurer in crossing deserts, seas and mountains, while avoiding a number of nasty traps set by the adversary.

2 A lesson with a simple adventure

Adventures have much the same potential in language learning as other simulations – they can generate a lot of enthusiastic and communicative oral language as learners work in groups (or as a whole class) towards the solution, and can form the basis for various oral and written post-mortem activities. As an example, we will look at a class using **Flash Rogers**,[2] a very simple adventure game which can be solved in a single lesson.

The task is for Flash Rogers (the player/hero) to rescue Susie Starlet (the helpless victim) from the evil King Kong, who has kidnapped her and taken her to his island castle. The rescue will involve finding a plane, flying safely over mountains of different heights, putting out a fire on board, shooting the villain, and getting into his castle.

At the beginning of the lesson, the teacher elicits or explains any useful vocabulary (in this case words like *runway, unlock, hangar,*

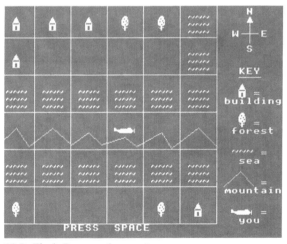

10.2 Flash Rogers: the magic map...

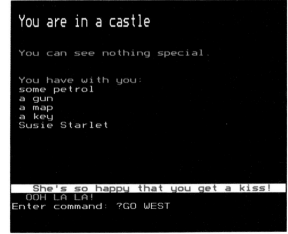

10.3 ...Success at last.

altitude), explains the situation, and gives out a simple paper grid for learners to keep a record of their movements. The learners then work in groups, each group with its own computer. If the class has never done an activity of this kind before, it may be necessary to give some hints about the limited 'grammar' the program understands.

They begin by exploring the terrain: the adventure is divided up into 'squares', and they move from one to another by typing **Go north** or **Go east**. In one square (a house) a group finds a gun, and decides to take it along (**Take gun**). Another discovers a map in a forest (**Take map**), but it is only later in the game that they realise, when lost, that they need to use it. But how? After a little experimentation, they try **Read map**, and the screen displays a 6 x 6 map of the adventure, which shows not only the route to the island and the relative heights of the mountains, but also magically shows them which square they happen to be in. (See Fig. 10.2.)

Another group overhears them, and tries the same command – only to discover that **You aren't carrying a map**! Other useful possessions include petrol, water and a key, and each of these must be found and 'taken' before they can be used.

Even a simple adventure such as this has hidden dangers. The students in one group, once in the plane, which they find in a hangar, press the + key to take off, and crash the plane into the roof of the hangar: they should have moved out of the hangar before they took off. In a later incarnation, after landing safely on the island, they come face to face with King Kong, but unfortunately have not found and taken the gun they will need if they are to survive till the next move.

Eventually, one of the groups, after a few false starts, succeeds in getting into the castle, rescuing the heroine (see Fig. 10.3), and flying her home. On reaching home, the hero proposes marriage, and the program produces a randomly generated **Yes** or **No**. The noise attracts the attention of other groups, who quickly recruit the winners to help them complete the adventure.

The lesson has lasted about fifty minutes, during which there has been constant conversation, as learners argue, suggest, criticise, hypothesise and explain. The teacher, too, has been busy. He has been going from group to group, helping the discussion on its way and giving hints when needed. For those who finish early and are not recruited into other groups, there is a question sheet which can be used as a basis for further writing and discussion. Questions include:

1   How many times did you get killed during the adventure. What happened?

2   What is the importance of each of the following in the adventure?
(a) petrol   (d) the map
(b) the key   (e) the gun
(c) water

3   Indicate on the diagram where you found each of them. Also show the position of the airport building, the hangar, the house, the forests and the castle.

4 Give directions on how to fly the plane safely.

5 What happened at the end of the adventure? Type GOTO 8000 and press RETURN. Did you get a different answer? If not, try again until you do. (This question relates to Susie's answer to the marriage proposal.)

If time is short, the question sheet can be used next lesson, or as the basis for a written homework. An obvious and useful follow-up to any adventure is a written narrative in the past tense telling the story of the adventure and how the player solved it.

An unexpected spin-off of a simple adventure is that it can be used to generate an information-gap activity, the gap being between learners who know the adventure and those who do not. The authors were wary about using **Flash Rogers** with a class in which a few of the students had already used the adventure in the school's computer club. Surely they wouldn't want to go through all that again? It turned out, however, that learners (like the rest of us) are delighted at the chance to demonstrate their knowledge and skill. Far from being bored, they were much in demand as informants and advisers, and their presence added a whole new dimension to the off-screen discussion.

3 Using longer adventures

It is unfortunate that so far, few adventure games have been written especially for language learning. As a result the language teacher wishing to use adventures with a class is forced to look at commercial adventures produced for the leisure market and aimed at (usually young) native speakers. In the search for suitable material, two things become clear. First, many adventures are too outlandish in content and/or vocabulary requirements: orcs, trolls, witches and magic spells do not figure highly in the General Service List. And second, commercial adventures are designed to last for some time: most will take anything from a week to six months to solve, which is reasonable from the point of view of the customer who has to pay upwards of £10 for the program.

The first problem puts many adventures out of consideration, though there are good reasons for using, say, **The Hobbit** with students who have read Tolkien's book and know what to expect.

The length and complexity of an adventure, however, does not prevent it from being used in class, given adequate preparation. Dr Armando Baltra[3] has described a novel and workable way of using a typical adventure program with language learners. The program is **Mystery House**, an adventure concerning hidden treasure, which Baltra chose partly because its lexis – the parts of a house, candle, hammer, matches, and so on – was within reasonable limits.

After becoming thoroughly familiar with the program (and no doubt 'dying' many times in the attempt), Baltra broke down the solution into smaller, solvable, one-lesson tasks, and explicitly assigned one to each of the groups in his class. In lesson one, for example, group one had to explore the ground floor, group two the upper storey and group three looked around the grounds outside. In addition, each group was told to look out for a 'source of light'. After a while, 'dusk' falls, and the computer reports that **You can't see anything**. At this point, the groups get together and compare notes, and another meaningful information-gap activity takes place as the information obtained separately by the different groups is pooled for the benefit of all – especially the location of the light source, which will be needed to continue adventuring through the 'night'.

The adventure continues in this fashion, with groups working separately under the teacher's guidance, and occasionally comparing notes. Naturally, students occasionally get stuck, and if the obstacle is a difficult one, the flow of the class (and the students' motivation) could suffer. (One of the authors spent rather more than two weeks getting past that snake in **The Wizard and the Princess**.) To avoid such situations arising, Baltra prepared written clues (often riddle-like, in simple rhyming couplets) which he handed out to groups who were stuck. This simple but elegant idea not only kept up the pace of the activity, but added a dimension lacking in the original program.

There is no way, however, that a class is ever going to finish a commercial adventure game in one lesson: the whole thing might take twelve lessons or more, even with help. Fortunately, there is a way of using an adventure periodically without starting from scratch each time: commercial adventures nearly always have a 'save' feature that enables you to store on disk or cassette your current position in the adventure, and then carry on from there the next time. An adventure used in this way becomes a 'serial', rather like a class reader which is used regularly over several weeks. Or, if time is short and you have the facilities, you could have an introductory lesson to an adventure like **Mystery House**, and then allow students to continue on a self-access basis at their leisure.

4 The sub-standard language of adventure games

Some teachers have expressed worry over the sub-standard English used in adventure games – **Take rock, Look room, Go plane.** This is understandable, but only becomes a problem if one regards the language input at the keyboard as the main language-learning element in an adventure. In fact, the value of a computer adventure game lies essentially in its use as a stimulus – for discussion, for planning, for later narration. The useful language is very much off-screen.

It is, conceivably, useful for students to type **Go south**, if they are learning the points of the compass, but most adventure games allow a simple **S** instead, and this should not be concealed from the students in the belief that it is 'good for them' to type **Go south**. The point of the command is to get them to another location, not to practise their spelling; other programs, designed for the purpose, can make a better job of this.

Adventure programs are in any case becoming more sophisticated linguistically, and there are already some that can understand inputs as complex as **Put the apple in the box** or even **Ask Gandalf politely** (Gandalf is not co-operative if the adverb is omitted). Two notable programs of this kind are **Zork** and **The Hobbit**, and more are undoubtedly on the way. This advance in the computer's ability to understand natural language is immensely important for CALL in general, as we shall see in Chapter 13, but less so in the realm of adventure games:

the point of an adventure, after all, is to play it, not so much to practise 'input' language in pseudo-conversation with the machine.

5 Multiple-choice adventures

Some adventures avoid the whole problem of 'natural language input' by relying on a multiple-choice approach: in this, they are similar to the mazes mentioned in Chapter 5, though more elaborate. **London Adventure**, which is specially designed for learners of English, puts the learner in the position of a tourist in London with a number of tasks to fulfil: exchanging money, sightseeing, buying postcards, and so on. The learner uses a menu of choices to decide where to go, and when language is called for, selects what he considers to be the most appropriate from a number of utterances. Thus, at a kiosk that sells postcards, if the learner tries to buy some by selecting **I like this postcard** (rather than **I'd like this postcard**) the postcard-seller says **Yes. It is nice**, and turns away to serve another customer. This adventure is unusual in having an inbuilt language-teaching element. (See Figs. 10.4 and 10.5.)

10.4 Trying to buy a postcard in London Adventure.

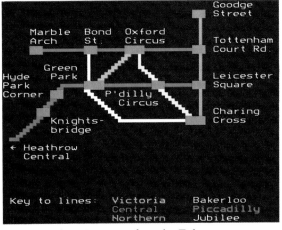

10.5 ...and getting around on the Tube.

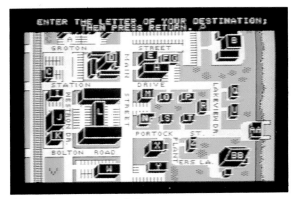

10.6 Felony: a map of the town...

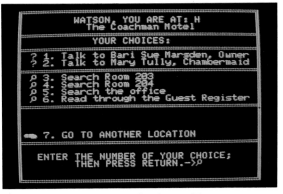

10.7 ...Inspector Watson decides on his next move.

Another multiple-choice adventure is **Felony**, in which the learner is given a number of crimes to solve. As the investigating officer, he is given a background to the case (either on screen or on paper) and a map of the town (see Fig. 10.6), and can visit any location on the map (scene of the crime, police station, hotels, parks, private homes, and so on) by pressing the appropriate key. Once there, he can choose among a number of options (**Interview X, Interview Y, Search the house**). (See Fig. 10.7.) The result is that several *clue numbers* appear on screen: these relate to items in a book of clues which contains several hundred clues in a jumbled order, relating to all twelve cases on the disk. The detective makes notes, and continues from option to option, and location to location, until he feels he can confidently name the guilty party and provide proof. Only one accusation is allowed, and that must be made within the (fictional) time limit specified by the program. The program has some nice touches, one of which is the fact that a reasonable amount of 'time' must elapse before the detective gets access to the post-mortem results. Another is a facility that allows up to four detectives to work on the case at the same time (taking it in turns to unearth clues), which makes it suitable for use in classes with only one machine.

6 Conclusion

Like all simulations, adventures involve the teacher in careful preparation and classroom management, if the most is to be made of them. They are, however, powerful motivators, and can bring into the classroom both exotic and more realistic scenarios, which can stimulate both oral communication and written follow-up activities.

Especially intriguing is the fact that *authoring programs* exist that allow users to create their own adventures. Using programs like **The Last Adventure, The Quill** and **Adventure Master**, learners can design their own adventure scenarios and plots for other learners to solve. These can be added to the list given in Chapter 8 of programs that can stimulate students to write in English.

11

The computer and listening

1 Introduction

Two areas of computer science that are of great potential relevance to language learning are *speech synthesis* and *speech recognition*. Speech synthesis chips are already used in arcade games, 'Speak 'n' Spell'[1] games, and in some makes of car which give the driver a spoken warning that, say, his brake fluid is running low. Speech recognition, conversely, allows a user to give a computer spoken commands: its uses include programs for industrial stock-taking, which allow the user to stroll around a stock-room speaking the names of the various items into a microphone.

Fascinating though these techniques are, they are not yet at a stage of development where they are of much direct use to the language learner. Most voice synthesisers are devoid of stress or intonation, and cannot compare with a human voice recorded on a cassette tape. And if voice synthesis is difficult, comprehension of human speech by the machine is much more so: the majority of programs that do exist have severely limited vocabularies, and can only 'understand' clearly uttered single words, and even then only when spoken by the same person who provided the original model utterance. Those programs that can go beyond this are prohibitively expensive, and require large amounts of computer memory. And although the field is developing fast, we are (some would say fortunately) a long way away from the time when a learner can sit down at a microphone and try out the latest language functions in an unplanned, informal chat with the computer.

There are, however, much simpler ways in which the computer can help learners to develop listening skills, which use cassette recordings (instead of voice synthesis chips) for the learner to listen to, and the keyboard (rather than the learner's voice) for his responses. The cassette recorder can be controlled separately from the computer or, given a suitable add-on such as the Tandberg AECAL cassette machine, can be operated via the computer, with either the learner or the program itself in control.

In the sections that follow, we will look at three areas that involve listening: ear-training (with a digression into pronunciation skills), general listening comprehension, and specific skills such as dictation and note-taking.

2 Recognising sounds

Learning to recognise and distinguish the sounds of a language is a prerequisite both for effective listening comprehension and for good pronunciation. As different nationalities have different problems with the sound systems of foreign languages, learners in multi-lingual classes will benefit most from individualised work on their particular problems, and the combination of a computer and a cassette recorder is a very good way of tackling this kind of work.

A sample exercise

As an illustration, we will imagine a learner doing a diagnostic ear-training test that uses minimal pairs (or minimal threes). The program tells him to start the cassette recorder, which provides him with a number of test items covering a variety of common problem areas. The program is a simple multiple-choice test: for each question on the cassette, the possible words or phrases appear on the screen, and the learner selects the one he thinks he has heard. He can, of course, hear the question as many times as he wishes by rewinding the cassette and playing it again. Besides giving instant feedback and keeping a score, the computer can keep a record of the *kinds* of error made by the learner, and on the basis of these recommend him to go on to suitable remedial programs.

Such ear-training exercises need not be limited to minimal pairs. Recognition of word and sentence stress can be practised by exercises asking learners to identify the stressed syllable(s) in recorded utterances; recognition of intonation patterns can be tested by asking learners to decide whether the voice they have heard is rising or falling at specific points; comprehension of the attitudinal aspects of intonation can also be practised in the same way.

Before leaving this exercise type, we should note the advantages gained by using the computer-controlled AECAL system instead of a free-standing cassette recorder:

1   It makes life easier for the learner: the cassette will start and stop as the program requires, removing the need for the learner to press the pause button constantly. Moreover, if he wants to hear an item again, he need only press the appropriate key and the recorder will automatically and almost instantly rewind to the right place and replay the item.

2   It can lead to better feedback: if the cassette plays *tongue*, for example, and the learner thinks he has heard *tang* (the other possibility being *tong*), the computer will respond by printing **No, 'tang' sounds like this**, and wind the cassette to the word *tang* (or a sentence featuring the word *tang*). It will then replay the target word *tongue* and ask the learner to try again.

3   It can make the program more flexible: in a long exercise with a variety of contrasts, the computer can be programmed to omit an item-type if the learner shows that he has mastered it (by getting, say,

three consecutive right answers with that particular type). Because the computer controls the tape, it can make it jump forward (or, indeed, backward) to any item it wants. This also makes possible a program that decides among choices *randomly*, and will therefore produce a different test each time it is used.

Pronunciation and intonation

As effective sound discrimination is essential before learners can hope to speak well, recognition practice goes hand in hand with practice in pronunciation and intonation. Much of the conventional practice of this type takes the form of 'listen-and-repeat' exercises conducted with a cassette recorder or in the language laboratory. Such exercises, however, have a fundamental weakness, in that a learner who fails to reproduce an item accurately has no way of knowing that this is the case: there can be no 'answer sheet' to which he can refer. If he cannot *hear* any difference between the model utterance and his own, he will continue to speak badly, and the exercise will merely serve to reinforce his bad habits.

There is a way in which the computer can improve this situation, using a technique involving *digitised speech*. Although computers are not very good at *understanding* the spoken word, they are able to analyse different sound patterns and distinguish them from each other. Given a suitable piece of add-on equipment, a computer can 'hear' an utterance spoken into a microphone, convert it into a digital form, store it on disk, and even reproduce the sound through a loudspeaker.[2] It can also be programmed to represent various aspects of the sound graphically on screen.

This capability can be used to good effect for intonation practice. One of the few systems so far available for microcomputers, **Visispeech**,[3] allows the teacher to say a phrase into a microphone. The computer displays its intonation curve, and the learner's attempt to copy the model is then displayed underneath. (See Fig. 11.1.) The learner is thus able to *see* the difference between the two, and experiment with different responses in an attempt to get as near a match as possible. The program gives the all-important feedback which the language laboratory exercise

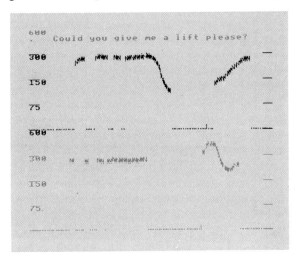

11.1 Visispeech: teacher's and student's intonation patterns.

lacks. As well as intonation, **Visispeech** can analyse an utterance in terms of voiced and unvoiced sounds, and relative volume.

Unfortunately, storing, analysing and displaying digitised speech is costly in memory and requires sophisticated programming techniques, and for these reasons more sophisticated programs than the one described above – programs which will also display pronunciation features – have as far as we know only been implemented on mini- and mainframe computers. However, things are developing fast, and it is hoped that as microcomputers with larger memories come on the market suitable programs will begin to appear.

3 Listening comprehension

One of the simplest ways of giving practice in listening comprehension is to use a multiple-choice or fill-in program in conjunction with a cassette recorder. The set-up is similar to the minimal pairs exercise, but uses comprehension questions instead of sound discrimination items. In addition to the normal feedback given after a wrong answer, the computer can offer to let the learner hear the relevant part of the tape again: with a separate cassette recorder, the 'error message' can give the learner appropriate counter numbers, or, if an AECAL is being used, the computer can automatically rewind to the right place.

Another, equally simple, technique is to use a tape in conjunction with a text-reconstruction program. We saw an example of this in Chapter 5 in the **Storyboard Plus** activity, in which learners reconstructed on screen a summary of a recorded anecdote, using the tape as an extra 'help' feature. Again, there would be advantages to be gained by using a computer-controlled cassette machine: the learner could opt to listen to any part of the anecdote at any time, but could not get 'lost', as the computer would prevent the tape from rewinding past the beginning of the story or winding past the end.

Such exercises not only help to integrate listening and writing skills, but also evaluate learners' listening comprehension skills in a more active and interesting way than is generally possible in a class lesson. In addition, if the work is done in groups and communication within the group is carried out in English, learners will gain valuable practice not only in listening to a cassette but also in listening to each other.

Variety in listening comprehension

We will now look at two activities which exploit the possibilities offered by the computer-controlled cassette recorder: **Picture Dictation** and **Getting the Message**.

Picture Dictation was devised as a demonstration program for a listening comprehension authoring package called **Mastwriter**. The learner is shown on the screen the outline plan of a bedroom, including windows and a door, with the letters **A** to **E** indicating the location of various pieces of furniture. He listens to a recording which tells him where each piece of furniture is. He is then asked, for example, **Where is the bed?**, and has to enter one of the letters. If he is correct, he goes on to the next question; if not he is given the chance to hear again the particular extract of the recording dealing with the position of the bed, the computer rapidly locating and playing the relevant section. The instructions for operating the program, the questions themselves and the error messages are also recorded on the tape, and these are automatically located by the program as required.

The second program, **Getting the Message**,[4] puts learners in the situation of being asked by a friend to take telephone messages for him while he is away. Some of the messages have been recorded on an answering machine, others have to be taken down from the person who is phoning. For example, there is a message from the friend's garage, telling him that his car, a blue Metro, registration FLX 142Y, which is being repaired after an accident, will be ready on Saturday morning and that the bill will be £110.40. The learners make notes of the relevant facts, and the AECAL enables them to listen to the recording again if they wish. (See Figs. 11.2 and 11.3.)

They then have to complete a gap-filling exercise, furnishing information such as the make, colour and registration number of the car, when it will be ready for collection and the cost of the repairs. For each gap in the text they have the option of entering an answer, listening to the relevant part of the recording again (i.e. *only* the section where the colour of the car is mentioned, or *only* the section when the collection date is given), or of 'cheating up' the answer. Later in the exercise their friend will 'ring' them and they will have to answer any questions he has about the car. These answers, which are based on the notes taken earlier, are given *orally*, using a microphone, and are recorded onto the tape. The program has already reserved a part of the tape to store the responses, which can later be played to the teacher.

There is a wide variety of exercises and contexts in **Getting the Message**. Learners have to remember to feed the cat: if they forget there is a recording of a plaintive *miaow*. And in order to feed the cat they have to listen to the instructions about where the cat food is kept. They take a message about an invitation to a party: there is apparently some confusion about the date of the party, which is sorted out when the girl who is giving it phones with an explanation and invites the learners to the party as well. A certain amount of diplomacy has to be used, since the friend's relations must not be told that he has had a car accident.

4 Dictation

Dictation has for some time been an unfashionable activity as far as general language teaching is concerned. We noted at the end of Chapter 3, however, that attitudes towards otherwise unpopular exercises can change when they are made available for self-access work on the computer, and the same may well be true of dictation. Be that as it may, there is no doubt that practice in dictation is valuable for those whose job involves this skill, particularly if the practice uses the appropriate medium: a keyboard.

It is not really practicable to develop a microcomputer program capable of satisfactorily marking a long piece of continuous writing, and the advantages of using a computer for this kind of work lie, in general, elsewhere. One program, however, avoids this problem by simply preventing mistakes from being entered.[5] The learner decides at the outset either to work from a 'blank page' or to call up a Storyboard-like 'map' of

11.2 *Getting the message: controlling AECAL via the computer keyboard...*

11.3 *...and listening to fill the gaps.*

the text, and then starts the cassette. The text is typed from beginning to end, correct letters appearing in place on screen, wrong ones only generating a faint hiss.

Three kinds of help are available: the next letter, the next whole word, or (temporarily) the whole text. At the end, the learner is given a breakdown of his performance (the number of times each 'help' feature was used, plus the number of wrong letters typed) and a rating based on a combination of all these factors (but making allowance for a certain number of typing rather than listening errors). The program, which works with a student-operated cassette recorder, would benefit considerably from being adapted to AECAL.

Another approach, and one which reflects the reality of the office for the ESP student, is to use a word-processor-like program with an AECAL recorder. The learner pays attention to layout as he types, controls the tape as he likes, and is free to leave out difficult bits and come back to them later. One 'help' function could be a specially constructed list of words whose spellings are likely to prove difficult. When the document is finished, it can be printed out and compared with a model answer previously stored on the disk. The difficulty of the dictation task will, of course, vary with the level of the learner: one interesting variation, which again involves both listening and writing skills, would be a letter dictated only in outline by a 'boss', leaving the 'secretary' to fill in the details, as so often happens in real life.

Other kinds of listening activity are possible for ESP students. Students of English for Academic Purposes, for example, could benefit from computerised practice in note-taking, perhaps using an AECAL hooked up to a word-processor.

Finally, for learners whose work involves acting upon spoken instructions, some interesting possibilities suggest themselves in the form of simulation programs linked to an AECAL recorder. The learner's success in, say, bringing a boat into harbour, would depend entirely on his successful comprehension of the instructions issued by the tape.

5 Video, compact disks and authoring

The whole area of listening and CALL is one which is undergoing rapid development. Of major interest are computer-controlled video recorders (both videodisk and videocassette-based), which give the same kind of control over film material as the AECAL gives over audiotape. Although not much usable material has yet been produced at a price schools can afford, some interesting work is going on, for example at Brighton Polytechnic, which has developed comprehension materials for the BBC's **Bid for Power** video. Also of interest are two pilot interactive video programs produced by Eurocentres: one, **Getting the Message**, is a video version of the program described earlier in this chapter, while the other, **Danger Mission**, is a video adventure designed specifically for learners of English.[6]

A related development is the *compact disk*, which has two major advantages over cassette: first, it can access data (sound, video or computer data) instantly, without even the short rewinding delay that AECAL entails; and second, a compact disk can store vast amounts of data compared with a cassette tape (or floppy disk). The combination of these two features has major implications for CALL. One is that a much greater variety of spoken response can be offered to learners. Another is that the large amount of space needed to store digitised speech ceases to be a problem. Whereas a typical floppy disk can store perhaps twenty digitised utterances intended for pronunciation practice, a compact disk can store hundreds.

But compact disks have their disadvantages too. With video and sound cassette tapes, teachers can create their own CALL listening materials – including their own video and sound recordings – using authoring programs. At the moment, however, amateurs can only *play* compact disks, not record onto them: recordings have to be made by professionals, and are expensive to produce. This may leave teachers at the mercy of technical experts who need large sales to cover high production costs. The results will be very polished, but may not be what language learners need.

6 Conclusion

Listening activities that use the computer are necessarily more complex than many other kinds of CALL materials, as they involve equipment other than the computer itself. As we have seen, this might be a simple cassette recorder, an AECAL recorder, or some kind of speech-digitising add-on.

As is always true with CALL, the complexity of what is happening beneath the surface does not necessarily mean that programs are difficult to use. On the contrary, learners readily take to devices like the computer-controlled tape recorder. Producing materials for learners is more time-consuming, as the teacher has the tape to cope with as well as the software, but a good authoring system can manage much of the complexity for him.

On balance, the advantages gained by using computers for listening practice in terms of variety, integration of skills, feedback and individualisation, make any extra complexity well worthwhile.

12

The computer as information source

We have already seen some ways in which the computer can be used in the language classroom as a source of facts and figures, rather like a reference book. In Chapter 7, for example, we talked about *spelling checkers* that automatically check the spelling in texts produced by learners on a word-processor. The list of words stored on the spelling checker disk, which can be expanded whenever necessary, forms what is called a *database*, a collection of facts or figures.[1]

In Chapter 4, on vocabulary, we described another database: a do-it-yourself dictionary, **Wordstore**, which enables learners to store new lexis on disk. In **Wordstore** the database consists of all the keywords entered into the program, together with their definitions and context sentences. (See Figs. 12.1 and 12.2.)

As these two examples suggest, databases come both as empty authoring programs that allow the user to store whatever information he likes, and as ready-made collections of information.

Their usefulness for language learners, therefore, is twofold. First, as we saw with the school information service described in Chapter 8, they can form the basis of writing activities: the writing, organisation and entering of data is itself a demanding and creative activity. Second, they can provide information for a variety of purposes, such as research for a project. In general databases, like word-processors, are best used when both functions are integrated: that is, when the data written on them by the learner is of real use as information to other learners.

In the sections that follow, we will look at three kinds of database, and ways in which they can be used: *student-compiled databases, disk-based ready-made databases* and *large commercial databases*.

2 Creating a database

Before going on to look at database programs being used in class, we will need to have a clearer picture of their capabilities. Most important is the ability to *search* for information on a variety of *fields*, a field being a particular area of information. If, for example, you wanted to build up a database of students at a language school, you would probably want to include their surname, first name, language level, date of birth, home address, telephone number and next-of-kin. You may also wish to include information about exams taken and results, exams entered for, career aspirations and hobbies. Each of these types or areas of information is a field.

Using a commercial database program, you first 'set up' the different fields under headings, and then enter the relevant information for each student, which the program stores on disk. Having thus created your database, you can now search on any field, or, in other words, carry out analyses that would be much more time-consuming without the help of a computer. You can, for example, display or print onto paper, lists (in alphabetical order) of students who share hobbies, who have the same career aspirations, who live in the same area of town, or who have been entered for specified examinations. You can rearrange students by age or by exam results. You can print out class lists, pass lists – in short, any information that can be derived from the corpus of information contained in the database. The information only has to be entered once: after that, the computer will manipulate it and print it out as you wish. (See Fig. 12.3.) In this way, a database takes much of the drudgery and head-scratching out of the mechanical business of information processing.

3 Student-compiled databases

The ability to search on fields can be very useful in the language classroom. It would, for example, be a fascinating experiment to get a class of students to create a database like the one described above about themselves, as we will see later. We start, however, with a simple project whose results are of obvious use to language learners: the compilation of a database of simplified readers. [2]

The database can be compiled by one class over a period of, say, a term, or by several classes in a shorter time. Either way, it makes use of a 'book box' containing about 100 simplified readers at appropriate levels. The first task is to decide on appropriate fields for the database. These might end up as:

Title
Author
Series
Level of difficulty (from 1 to 10)
Fiction/non-fiction
Type of story (if fiction)
Subject matter (if non-fiction)
Rating (from 1 to 10)
Comments
Read by

To get the database started, the teacher chooses a reader that the class has read together, or at least some students have read, and discusses with them what they want to say about it. Once agreement is reached, the information is fed into the computer as a database entry. The entry might read:

Title:	K's First Case
Author:	Louis Alexander
Series:	Longman Structural Readers
Level:	2
	Fiction—Detective story
Rating:	8
Comments:	A good story, with a clever ending.
	Where is K's Second Case?
Read by:	Hanna, Pierre, Ahmad, Silvia

Now that the structure of the database is established, it can begin to grow. Each student borrows and reads a different reader from the book box, then compiles an entry on paper, checks it with the teacher, and adds it to the database. Alternatively, groups of students can read the same reader, and discuss the more subjective fields before feeding in the agreed information.

If the class has fifteen or so students, it will not be long before the database starts to become usable as an information source. A student can,

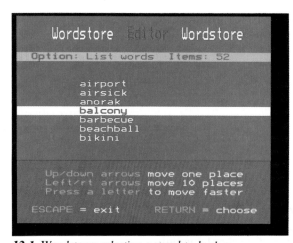

12.1 Wordstore: selecting a word to look up...

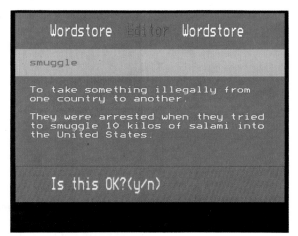

12.2 ...and adding a new entry.

```
        BEEBUG MASTERFILE II
    A.  Set up file name
    B.  Enter record description
    C.  Look at/alter a record
    D.  Printer configure
    E.  Open file
    F.  Initialise/Clear file
    G.  Enter search data
    H.  Print/Search file
    I.  Sort
    J.  Transfer/append files
    K.  Compact the file
    L.  Global field calculation
    M.  Activate'TAG'file
    N.  Utilities
    O.  Form design
    P.  Stop the program
    OPTION?
```

12.3 Masterfile: a database menu page.

for example, look up a reader before borrowing it, and will be particularly interested in its rating, and the 'review' given it in the *comments* section. Or he can ask the database to list the names of non-fiction readers at level 3 which have a rating of 5 or better, or detective fiction at any level.

There is a different post-reading task for students who choose books that are already on the database. As well as adding their name to the list of borrowers, they can challenge any part of the entry they disagree with: perhaps they enjoyed it more than the previous student, or want to add comments of their own. These questions can be discussed with the student or students who compiled the original entries, which may be changed as a result. And because the readers are used constantly, the database is never complete: there are always changes to be made, new books to add, and perhaps old ones to be deleted.

The benefits of an ongoing project of this sort are several. In the first place, learners are encouraged to read, in much the same way as they were encouraged to write in Chapter 8: the creation of the database helps to give the reading a real purpose. Second, the compiling of entries gives opportunities for genuine discussion and purposeful writing. And third, the resulting database is a useful source of information for learners, both on screen and on paper, and one which they will use with some satisfaction because they have created it themselves.

The above is only one of many projects that could be centred around a student-compiled database. Other topics might include well-known people in various fields, towns and cities, jobs and careers, and English language TV and radio programmes. In schools where an 'integrated curriculum' is in operation, a project could be devised that fitted in with work currently being done in other subject classes such as History, Geography or English Literature. Whatever the topic, the database can provide a *focus* for a variety of classroom activities.

We end this section with a more light-hearted database project, which was devised and managed by a group of ESP students who wanted the experience of creating a database in English. In a class 'brainstorming' session, they hit on the idea of a school computer dating service. After deciding on their fields (sex, age, complexion, likes, physique, and so on), they devised questionnaires for students to fill, and charged a small fee to put their details into the database. Here is the teacher's report, as it appeared in the school journal:

'I want a 19 year old Italian'
'Just find me anybody – I'm not fussy'
'I don't want anyone in my group'
'I got eleven men'

These were the kinds of remarks going around the Cambridge staffroom in the penultimate week of term. The B Unit computer group had a hit on their hands – computer dating at 50p a head.

Staff and students filled in two questionnaires. The first gave information about the student/staff members and formed part of the database; the second gave information about their Perfect Partner. About 130 names went into the database and about 100 looked for partners. Not everyone was happy with the computer's idea of 'perfect', but in general we had a lot of satisfied customers. Of course, what they did with the list of names was their own business!

The computer group had a good time devising the questionnaires, publicising the venture and generally disrupting the school for a week. The £85 raised will be given to charity.

Who says computers are boring?[3]

4 Using databases to classify school resources[4]

Before leaving the subject of 'authoring' databases, we should consider briefly the value of using a database to classify not just simplified readers but all the language-teaching resources in a school. This could include whole books, individual parts of books, worksheets, audiocassettes, videocassettes, flashcards, films and, of course, computer programs. Useful fields would be:

- the *location* of the material (e.g. the library, language laboratory, learning centre)
- the *level* (e.g. elementary, intermediate)
- *language functions* (e.g. narration, regretting, basic greetings)
- *structure content* (e.g. simple past, location prepositions)
- *skill* (e.g. grammar practice, listening comprehension) and
- *topic* (e.g. sport, London, food).

It then becomes possible to print out lists of materials at a particular level, or dealing with a particular topic, or a specific grammatical area. Teaching materials can thus be identified and located easily: a much better situation than finding that it is quicker to write materials again than to locate them.

Such lists can also be used by students, and can be posted in learning centres, computer rooms and self-access language laboratories. If they are recommended, either by a teacher or as the result of some diagnostic test, to do some more work on, say, the present perfect continuous, it is very useful for them to be able to consult a central index which lists appropriate exercises at a variety of levels and in a variety of media such as audiocassette, worksheet or computer program.

The taking of paper printouts means that it is unnecessary to have the database 'up and running' (and therefore stopping the computer from being used for other things). It can, of course, be accessed for special requests, and for updating. And as it is updated, it is a simple matter to make new printouts to replace the old.

5 Ready-made databases

At the upper levels of language learning, work often takes the form of topic-based projects, lasting anything from a double lesson to several weeks. ESP students may, for example, want to investigate some economic aspect of Britain or another country, while the non-specialist language learner may prefer to concentrate on a topic such as entertainment, health or holidays. Such work will require a variety of source materials: audio and video tapes, articles and reference books. Ready-made disk-based databases are a useful addition to these resources, as they can provide particular information quickly, and in the form requested by the user.

As an example, an ESP group working on an economics project might want to make use of a program called **Regional Statistics**, which gives details of population, house ownership, jobs, salary and wage levels and ownership of consumer durables such as washing machines, refrigerators, cars and telephones in different parts of the UK. By browsing around the database and asking different questions, learners can draw conclusions about patterns of wealth, industry and employment.

Another program, **Macroeconomic Database**, gives details of national incomes and other relevant data on twenty-five countries for the period 1959-1981. It also includes a set of programs which help to manipulate the data and draw statistical conclusions. Users can enter their own information and thereby update the program. Again, much useful language practice can be had by formulating questions, suggesting strategies for interrogating the database, interpreting facts supplied by it and locating the information necessary to update it.

For the less specialist learner, there are, for example, a number of nutritional databases which could be used for a project on health and diet. Learners can get information about the nutritional value of different foods – vitamins, starch, fat content, and so on – and decide on suitable diets for people of different ages and different weights. With some programs, you can type in a meal, and the computer will give you a breakdown of its constituents – including the all-important calorific value. Interactional databases like these not only contribute information to a class project, but have an added motivational impact as well.

6 The world outside: larger databases

The amount of information held on disk-based databases is, of course, limited by the capacity of the disk. Given the right equipment, however, it is possible to gain access to much larger, commercial databases. In many countries, this can be done without a computer at all, via a specially adapted TV set. Using a keypad and the menu pages displayed on the TV screen, the user can browse through information about train and plane timetables, current exchange rates, TV, theatre or cinema programmes, news headlines, the weather forecast, and much, much more. This service, which was first mentioned in Chapter 8, is called *Teletext*.

It is easy to see how such information can be incorporated into a simulation or role-play. Students can use the database to plan a trip, consulting the plane and train timetables, comparing the time taken by each method of transport, finding out currency rates, seeing what the weather will be like, possibly changing their plane if the weather looks bad. And they will be stimulated by the knowledge that they are dealing with real and up-to-the-minute information.

Teletext is a 'passive' database: users merely consult it without being able to interact with it in any way. There are also interactive databases in Britain and elsewhere, held on mainframe computers which have a capacity many times greater than a micro. The information is accessed by linking the micro to the mainframe (which can be hundreds of miles away) by means of the telephone, using an add-on called a *modem*.

With a modem, the user not only has access to information: he can also *do* something with that information. He can, for example, consult train and plane timetables as with Teletext. More importantly, he can *book* a theatre or plane seat and *buy* a case of wine. Some control of both staff and students is therefore desirable.

The most widely known database of this type in Britain is **Prestel**. Some information pages can be consulted free of charge, often if they contain publicity of some kind; for others, containing more specialised information, a charge may be made. There is also a charge for using the telephone lines, and usually a charge to use the mainframe computer time. For the more specialised databases there will also be an annual subscription charge. So using such resources can be a costly business. It can, however, also be extremely stimulating.

It is, for example, possible to subscribe to a database which lists all books published in Britain since 1950 (**BLAISE: British Library Automated Information Service**), aiding project work not only in schools but also at graduate and postgraduate level.

DIALOG, operated by the Lockheed Corporation in the US, is the world's largest on-line information service with information on over 200 subjects as diverse as medicine, space, news and leisure. Yet it can be accessed at very reasonable cost, even from the UK.

There are various education-oriented databases available in Britain, including **Prestel Education**, and **The Times Network for Schools**, which contain information relating to both curricular and extra-curricular activities. In the words of the Times Network publicity material, users will be able to 'initiate research projects, enter competitions, send and receive programs, pool technical expertise and equipment, and find out about national and local events... Older students will be able to find out about different careers and apply for jobs directly through the system'.

Other facilities available through various databases, sometimes requiring a subscription, include *bulletin boards* and *electronic mail*. Using a bulletin board, learners can compose messages to be displayed on an 'electronic notice board', really just a number of pages, to be read, and possibly answered, by a potentially large and disparate audience. Electronic mail is a variation on the theme of bulletin boards: learners write messages to a particular addressee and send them over the phone line to his mailbox number for collection. The penfriend of the future?

7 Conclusion

We have looked at a number of different ways of exploiting databases in language learning. Their uses are, in fact, only limited by the imagination of the teacher and learners: as we saw earlier, groups of learners are quite capable of coming up with their own ideas, and of bringing them to fruition.

Whereas do-it-yourself databases can be purchased at very little expense, the cost of buying a modem and subscribing to commercial databases can be high. In a large institution, however, such facilities are useful elsewhere than in the language department, and there is no reason why the expense could not be shared among the various departments of the school.

13

Discovery and exploration

1 Introduction

In this chapter, we come to what is perhaps the most intriguing and, so far, the least developed area of CALL: the use of the computer as a medium for exploring language.[1] Two basic kinds of program exist, both of which require the computer to be 'intelligent'. In the first kind, the computer is provided with a rule or rules, which the learner attempts to discover by trying examples of his own. These programs are fairly simple to construct. Programs of the second type are more complex, and require the computer to understand not only rules, but also a situation: such programs allow the learner both to modify the situation and to engage in limited but natural 'conversation' with the computer about it.

Most of the work in this field has so far been done by John Higgins and Tim Johns, who are also the authors of most of the programs described below. The fact that these programs also appear in Higgins' and Johns' *Computers in Language Learning* (Collins, 1984) is evidence of how little the field has developed in the last few years, though it is hoped that as time goes on more exploratory programs will appear.

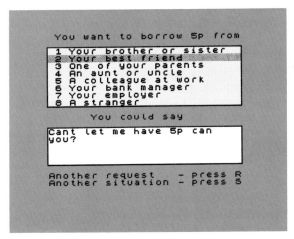

13.1 Loan: Asking for a small loan...

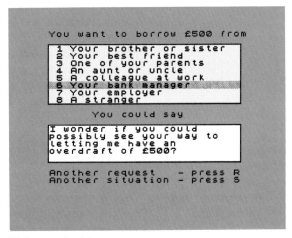

13.2 ...and a bigger one.

2 Finding the rule

The simplest discovery programs – so simple that our first two examples were written by Tim Johns for a 1K Sinclair ZX81 computer – deal with the rules of English morphology. **S-Ending** offers to display the plural (or third person singular) form of any noun or verb typed in by learners at the keyboard. As well as straightforward examples like *book/books*, the program can handle items like *fly/flies* (but without being caught by *key/keys*) and *punch/punches* (and, surprisingly, getting *loch/lochs* right too). It will, however, attempt to add an 's' to any string of letters typed in (including nonsense words), so it can be caught out by irregular plurals like *sheep* and mass nouns like *accommodation*.

A second program, **A/an**, offers to place either *a* or *an* before any word or phrase the learner types in. Again, the program is hard to catch out, as it will correctly produce, for example, both *an uninformed man* and *a uniformed man*.

A similar program exists for *-ing* endings,[2] and one could easily be devised for past endings, which would first scan a list of irregular verbs, then carry out the appropriate *-ed* (or other) modification.

A useful way of exploiting these programs is to allow groups of learners to try out their hypotheses at the keyboard, each group having a dictionary and grammar book that can be used to check the program's responses, then to discuss their findings in a whole-class session. Discussion would centre around the morphological rules discovered by learners while using the program, but would also include cases where the program got it wrong. It is important to realise here that it is not necessary for the program to be 100 per cent correct in its answers: the possibility of 'catching out' the machine can be a powerful motivator, and can lead to lively discussion. The need to check the machine's output in reference books also provides a good opportunity for learners to develop study skills.

This idea of 'checking on the machine' can be used to advantage with areas of language other than morphology, where the point of the exercise is for learners to evaluate the appropriateness of the machine's response. In **Loan** and **Apologies**,[3] learners can select from a range of situations and the machine will produce what it considers to be an appropriate way of either asking for a loan or apologising. By and large, the computer makes a reasonable effort (see Figs. 13.1 and 13.2), but as with all things functional, the choice of exponent is open to question. As with the previous examples, learners have the twofold task of attempting to discover the rules by which the program selected its utterances and keeping a critical eye on its performance. It would be possible to produce a range of programs dealing with a variety of other interactional functions such as greetings, suggestions, advice and criticism, which could all be used in much the same way.

3 The computer and natural language

One of the main thrusts of computer development over the past few years has been *artificial intelligence*, which, among other things, is concerned with enabling computers to understand and produce natural language. There are already a number of *expert systems* running on mainframe computers, that the user can interrogate using a restricted variety of ordinary English rather than pre-determined 'computer-speak' commands. Clearly, a program that could understand and respond intelligently to natural language inputs typed in by learners could be of immense benefit in language learning: the computer would become a patient and authoritative interlocutor that a learner could make use of whenever he chose to.

As always, things are not that simple. The ability to communicate freely in a natural language requires, among other things, a knowledge of the world that no computer could ever possess. A computer's linguistic ability, therefore, will necessarily be limited to the 'world' that it has been programmed to understand. This is the case with an expert system, which can understand things relating to its speciality, but nothing else.

This limitation should not discourage language teachers. On the contrary, much language teaching relies on precisely the kind of limited context or situation that a computer could be expected to cope with. It would be reasonable, for example, for a computer to be equipped with the language of giving directions and some kind of a town map: within the limits of the map, it would be competent to understand and give directions from one place to another, though it would not be able to talk about the weather, tell a story or answer queries about train departures. The program would have three main components: a *situation* component, in which the map and our position on it would be stored, a *language synthesiser*, enabling it to talk about that situation in English, and a *parser*, enabling it to understand English input by the learner.

In the remainder of this chapter, we look at some of the possibilities offered by 'intelligent' computer programs of this sort.

4 John and Mary

John and Mary is one of the very few CALL programs that allow natural language interaction between computer and learner. Although very simple in concept and limited in language range, it will serve to demonstrate the principles on which more elaborate programs could be based.

The program displays a room with an open door at the back (leading to a kitchen). Two stick figures represent John and Mary: John is standing in the room, Mary is visible through the open door. This is the 'situational' element of the program. What happens next is up to the learner. There are four possibilities:

1   He can make statements about what he sees on the screen, and the program will react to them. Thus **Mary is in the kitchen, The door is open** and **John and Mary aren't together** will all generate **I agree**, while **John is in the kitchen** will generate **I disagree**.

2   He can ask the program questions about the situation. The program understands both yes/no and wh- questions, and will answer them truthfully. If a question is asked that the program's parser cannot cope with, it will simply respond **I don't understand**.

3   By pressing RETURN, he can get the machine to generate well-formed and relevant questions of its own about the situation. These he can

answer himself, or he can get the machine to answer them by pressing RETURN again. Thus a learner can, if he so chooses, spend some time simply watching the machine ask and answer a whole series of different questions.

4 Most interesting, he can tell the machine to change the situation. If he types **Shut the door**, the screen will be redrawn with the door shut. If he then tries **Bring Mary into the lounge**, the machine responds with **The door's shut**, and the door will have to be opened again before the move can be accomplished.

The learner can switch between these four interactional modes at any time, and so can, for example, ask the machine a few questions, then change the situation around a little, ask it some more questions about the new situation, change it again, and finally get the machine to interrogate him. (See Figs. 13.3–13.5.)

13.3 John and Mary: asking the computer questions...   *13.4 ...answering the computer's questions...*

13.5 ...and changing the scenario.

94

In spite of its apparent simplicity, **John and Mary** can handle a variety of language areas: two types of question, together with their appropriate short answer forms; statements, imperatives, and the difference between *bring* and *take*. It could fairly be described as a program that deals with grammar, yet it does so in a very different way from the programs described in Chapters 2 and 3. Those programs set the learner problems to solve and awarded marks. **John and Mary** sets no tasks and awards no marks: it simply invites the learner to use language to explore a situation.

Higgins describes programs of this sort as belonging to *Grammarland*, a place analogous to Papert's *Mathland*, where learners can go to flex their grammatical muscles in a non-threatening environment. Unfortunately, *Grammarland* is so far a very restricted country, but it is worthwhile looking at some ways in which it might develop.

5 Other exploratory programs

Five Towns[4]

The 'world' of **Five Towns** is a 'county' in which the program places five towns in randomly chosen locations each time it is run. The program has a parser which enables it to understand and answer a variety of comparative questions – some quite complicated – about the positions of the towns. Thus it can answer, among other things, **Which is further north, Town A or Town B?** and even **Is Town B further from Town C than Town D is from Town A?**

The program is not intended as a candidate for *Grammarland*, but it could easily be made so: if it were able to generate its own questions for the learner to answer, it could be a very useful supplement to a unit of work on comparison. Even as it is, much could be gained from having it in the self-access room.

Giving directions

We mentioned earlier a more complex program with a geographical basis: one that could understand and produce the language of giving directions. Although such a program does not yet exist, as far as we know, it is easy to imagine how it might work and how it would be used by language learners. First the program would display a street plan of a small town, naming the streets and important buildings. The plan could be a representation of a real place, or, more interestingly, could be randomly generated by the machine, and therefore different each time the program was run. A variety of activities then become possible, along the lines of **John and Mary**:

1   The learner tells the machine to give directions from Point A to Point B, which it would print as a short paragraph. Because there are many ways of giving comprehensible directions, the machine will tend to give slightly different directions each time. The task could therefore be repeated, and the differences compared.

2   The machine asks the learner for similar directions. The learner enters his directions, one sentence at a time, and the machine responds by moving a blob around the town map as instructed.

3 The machine randomly selects and dictates a route around the town, one sentence at a time. The learner tests his comprehension by moving the blob himself (perhaps using the arrow keys or a joystick) in the directions indicated, and the machine keeps a check on his movements.

4 The learner simply watches as the machine dictates a route to itself, and follows its own instructions.

There is no doubt that this would be a difficult program to write, but it is perfectly feasible for a microcomputer to perform this kind of task. As a final hypothetical example, we will consider a slightly simpler program, this time with a situation described in words rather than pictures.

Personal information

This program would be equipped with a database of 'personal information' stored as lists of names, jobs, types of accommodation, names of cities, personal possessions, ages, hobbies, nationalities and descriptions of marital status. To begin with, it would select at random from these lists to create a fictional character, whom it would describe in a paragraph on the screen. The paragraph might look like this:

> **Cathy is Australian. She's twenty-seven, single, and lives in a flat in Sydney. She's an accountant, and works for a bank. She's got two dogs, and drives a BMW. She enjoys walking, music and water-skiing.**

In *Grammarland* fashion, the learner can interrogate the program – **How old is Cathy? What does she do for a living?** – or get the program to ask the questions. He could also change the scenario as he wished, by retyping a sentence. He could, for example, change her to a doctor working in a hospital, or an American living in Paris. Or he could ask the program to produce an entirely new scenario and proceed from there.

This last facility provides a severe test of the program's 'intelligence'. The program must know, for example, that whereas being an accountant and being a doctor are, in general, exclusive choices (since you are either one or the other), having two dogs and having a swimming pool are not. If faced with **She's a doctor**, therefore, the program would replace **accountant** with **doctor**, and alert the learner to the unlikelihood that a doctor should work in a bank. If, however, the learner types **She's got a swimming pool**, it would *add* this to her list of possessions. There would therefore have to be some kind of cutting-off point to prevent the paragraph from getting too long. The learner could, of course, perform his own censorship by typing some agreed convention such as **Cut music**, before adding a replacement hobby of his own choice.

6 Conclusion

There are good reasons why much of this chapter has been speculative. Programs of the *Grammarland* type are far from easy to write, and if they are to be flexible in their comprehension and production of language, require large amounts of computer memory and a truly dedicated programmer with independent financial means. While a multiple-choice program can be used to supplement almost any area of language learning, an exploration program with natural language capability, besides taking at least ten times as long to write, will, in the end, be restricted to the limited 'world' around which it was written. For the programmer, the reward does not as yet justify the effort.

The reward for the learner, however, in having a non-competitive 'linguistic playmate' on which new language can be tried, is potentially enormous, and for this reason it is to be hoped that more and better programs of this kind become available in the near future.

14

Summing up: the place of the computer

1 Introduction

In the preceding chapters we have seen the computer playing a number of roles in a wide variety of language-learning activities: quizmaster, games manager, simulator, workhorse, information source, 'intelligent' cassette controller and medium for exploration. We are now in a position to tie some theoretical and pedagogical threads together, before going on to the more practical concerns of CALL in Part 2.

As CALL tends to arouse strong feelings among language teachers, we begin with a discussion of attitudes towards computers, attitudes which are often influenced by experiences with a previous technological innovation in language learning: the language laboratory. We then look at the place of the computer in the language curriculum, and consider some problems of classroom management.

2 Attitudes towards computers

In the past twenty years or so, language teachers have been called upon to adopt a whole range of technical devices: teachers who themselves mastered a foreign language with the aid of nothing more technical than a book, blackboard and chalk are now expected to be able to use slide projectors, cassette recorders, overhead projectors, language laboratories, video recorders – and now computers. There is inevitably scepticism about whether all these aids are really needed, whether some are expensive gimmicks, to be discarded after a few years when novelty value has worn off.

Methods vs resources

In the minds of many teachers, computers are still inextricably linked to the idea of programmed learning: they are stuck with the image of rows of students hunched over computer keyboards, working alone and in silence at mechanical drills. The scenario is much the same as the traditional language laboratory, except that the answers are typed rather than chanted. Such teachers feel that labs have little relevance to communicative methods of language learning and that computers, after their initial popularity has waned, will go the same way as labs.

On the other hand, there are many teachers who find language laboratories very useful. They do not, however, force their students to work through endless grammar drills – though these are available if that is what the students wish to do – and see the lab as a *resource* to be exploited in a variety of ways, not as a dictator of one particular approach to language learning. They use it as a 'listening library', where students can listen to cassettes in the same way as they might read books in a library; where they can borrow cassettes to take home, as they might borrow books from a library; where they can choose from a large selection of cassettes dealing not only with grammar and pronunciation exercises but also stories, songs, news broadcasts (preferably of that day's news), weather forecasts (for that day), interviews, current affairs programmes, and radio features on a wide variety of subject matter. In other words, the lab has become a rich linguistic environment, where learners can be exposed to and increase their knowledge of the target language.

In such a laboratory, oral work still has a place, but it is far more communicative: instead of chanting repetitious drills, learners work in pairs on writing and recording dialogues; they listen to their recordings and analyse their performance; they re-record until they are satisfied, and ask the teacher to listen to their end product and make comments.

Because it is no longer necessary for the teacher to monitor and interrogate each learner via the microphone and headphones, the design of the laboratory can be changed. Learners need no longer sit in rows facing the teacher; working positions can be arranged in clusters around tables or around the edges of the walls. Because of developments in microphone and headphone technology, the old partitions separating learners and reinforcing the cell-like effect can be done away with.

This language laboratory has little in common with the lab of the sixties. The equipment is similar, in some cases identical: but the way in which it is used is very different. The language laboratory has become a medium that can be used with a variety of teaching methods and for a variety of purposes. It is no longer a method in its own right, nor is it inextricably linked to any one method.

It is this point that is relevant above all others to computers in language learning. As we have tried to demonstrate throughout this book, the use of computers is compatible with a variety of approaches, methods and techniques of learning and teaching. The computer is a resource: it is emphatically not a 'programmed-learning machine'.

Computer replaces teacher?

There are other ways in which computers and language laboratories are linked in many teachers' minds. In both cases, there were early fears that they would replace the teacher, that the teacher would become superfluous (as indeed there were when the BBC started its schools radio service in the 1920s). In the case of the language laboratory these fears proved groundless, but many teachers remain worried that the computer may oust them from the classroom, an opinion which is not shared by those who have experience of using computers with language learners.

Although fears of the computer as some kind of a rival were understandable in the fifties, when the prevailing behaviourist theories had reduced the teacher's role to mere drill-management, the arrival of communicative language learning has given the teacher a sure and lasting edge over any kind of mechanical or electronic 'tutor'. Nor have teachers in schools where CALL is used found themselves suddenly underemployed: on the contrary, as we have seen in earlier chapters, there is more work to do than ever.

Technophobia

Another common barrier to CALL is a fear among teachers of the technical aspects of computers, which finds voice in the claim that they are 'teachers, not technicians'. Such feelings are reinforced when demonstrations by enthusiastic amateurs (and sometimes professionals) go hopelessly wrong: the program will not load, or 'crashes' when the user innocently presses the wrong key. If the experts have trouble, the reasoning goes, how can I be expected to manage with a class of students?

This is a real enough problem. Programs can fail to load, especially if cassettes are being used rather than disks, and programmers do have a tendency to display their wares publicly before all the 'bugs' have been ironed out. With a combination of a well-written program and a disk-based system, however, problems are unlikely to arise. After switching on the computer, the teacher or learner need only press a couple of keys to get the program up and running. And as far as mechanical reliability is concerned, computers should come as a pleasant surprise to those who remember the constant breakdowns of early language labs. Most makes of computer are very reliable, and robust enough to withstand the constant use (and occasional misuse) they will have to undergo in the language classroom.

All this is not to say that CALL is problem-free. The newcomer will encounter pitfalls which can only be avoided with experience and training, as we will see in later chapters. But there is nothing intrinsically difficult about using computers, and no reason for the computer-illiterate teacher to feel nervous or inadequate.

The computer bandwagon

Just as harmful as uninformed prejudice against computers is its opposite: an uncritical enthusiasm for all things electronic. History reveals an alarming tendency in the language teaching profession to embrace wholeheartedly one method (or piece of technology) as 'the answer', only to reject it equally wholeheartedly for another as disillusion sets in. Victims have included, at different times, the use of the learner's mother tongue, the teaching of grammar, drills, the use of labels and explanations, and the language lab. Those who tell us that the non-computerised lesson is in some way inadequate should be firmly resisted: they will be the first to abandon computers for some other bandwagon as time goes on.

Equally, we should beware of dogmatism within CALL, which insists that one particular use of the computer is its only 'proper' role in language learning. It can take many forms. One is that any program without graphics and sound 'fails to utilise the full potential of the machine'. Another is the claim that the computer should be used only for word-processing, or only for drills, or only for simulations. Such narrow views can only do harm, as they deny the computer's potential as a flexible resource, and claim a false identity between machine and method.

3 Using the computer

How, then, should this resource be used, and how does it fit into the general language curriculum? The answer to this question will depend ultimately on the individual teacher, his students, and the space and number of computers available, but there are a number of general principles that can be stated.

Planning a lesson

Like any other teaching aid, the computer is only effective if it is used as part of an overall lesson plan. The teacher should have a clear idea of the purpose of the lesson within the overall programme of studies, and the role he wants the computer to play in achieving that purpose. Although it can be tempting to regard the computer as some kind of substitute teacher, computers cannot organise and run a lesson any more than a cassette recorder or a coursebook can: the important thing about all these resources is how they are exploited. And as the most flexible classroom aid available to language teachers, computers demand correspondingly more careful thought if they are to be used to the best advantage.

The teacher who complains that the novelty value of CALL is wearing off, and that his students now only want to use computers for one lesson in twenty instead of one lesson in ten, is probably expecting the machine to do all the work. In all likelihood, he is either treating the computer lesson as a 'Friday afternoon fun session', or as a free period in which he 'plugs the students in' in the good old language lab fashion and forgets all about them.

Integrating the computer with the curriculum

Work with computers is not an end in itself: the more it is integrated with normal classroom work, the more relevant it will be – and the more relevant the learner will perceive it to be. In this respect, authoring programs are invaluable, as they allow the teacher to tailor the content of CALL activities to the learners' current needs, be they grammatical, lexical or text-based. Writing with a word-processor should be writing that learners would normally be doing at that stage of the course. Simulations should be chosen that give learners opportunities to use language they have recently acquired.

Just as computers should not be seen in isolation from the normal curriculum, nor should they be isolated from other classroom resources. We have seen computers being used alongside dictionaries and other reference books, and together with cassette recorders. Treating the computer as just another teaching aid will not only help to dispel any nervousness felt by learners about using computers, but will also encourage them to make better use of all the resources available to them.

Variety in CALL

We have seen that computers are much more than question-and-answer machines, and their potential for variety should be exploited. Although the inexperienced teacher would be well advised to start with fairly simple and 'safe' programs, such as vocabulary games or text-rebuilding exercises, he will soon be confident enough to try more ambitious activities that make use of simulations and word-processors.

Nor is there any need to limit himself to the activities described in Chapters 2–13. The field of CALL is relatively new, and there is plenty of scope for experiment and innovation. There is, for example, a large amount of business software that could be well exploited with ESP classes, given some imagination: this includes accountancy, spreadsheet and stock control programs. Some schools, too, run word-processing clubs outside classroom hours, and computer clubs in which students can learn to program computers themselves: the results can be surprisingly good, and can even provide material for later language classes.

Self-access CALL

If a school is lucky enough to have a number of computers and a spare room, every effort should be made to make them available on a self-access basis. The computer room (which is dealt with in detail in Chapter 17) can be stocked with a library of supplementary software – both 'authored' software and 'dedicated' programs bought in for the purpose – and machines can be booked by interested learners.

Self-access CALL is important for several reasons. First, it gives the *learner* the chance to choose what he wants to do. He may want to follow up recent classwork, update his personal dictionary, do remedial exercises, write letters or just play with the machine: it's up to him. Second, it makes computers available to those who want them, without forcing them on everyone: some learners will be there every afternoon, others once a week, and some not at all. And third, it may be the only access to computers the learner has: if classroom time is short, as is often the case, the teacher may have to be content with recommending suitable CALL programs for students to use in their own time. Self-access CALL is better than no CALL at all.

How much CALL?

Computers, like anything else, can be overused. Although we have been concerned to demonstrate the capabilities of the computer in a number of fields, this is not to say that it has to be used for all of these purposes all of the time. It is better for a teacher to feel frustration at not having the time to exploit the computer to the full, than to feel any obligation to fit it into every single lesson. However fascinating teachers and learners may find CALL, the computer is, after all, only a tool, and this is reflected in the frequency with which it is used in the language classroom. Even in language schools that are well-equipped with computers, learners rarely use them for more than one or two classroom hours a week out of a total programme of twenty hours or more. If well planned, however, those one or two hours can prove to be an extremely valuable and motivating addition to the programme of studies. And if machines are available for self-access work as well, so much the better.

4 Classroom management

We have seen computers being used in three basic modes: by individuals, by groups and by the whole class. Which of these modes the teacher uses most will depend on the number of computers available, which can range from one per school to one per learner. Although we feel that the ideal number is one machine for every three class members, plus at least one in the staffroom reserved for teachers, there is much that can be done with only one computer. The tactics, however, will necessarily differ.

If there is only one computer available for the whole school it is often a good idea to make it available for self-access by students and teachers. In this way both staff and students can gradually get to grips with the machine and ways in which it can be exploited. Teachers are not forced to demonstrate in front of a whole class of critical students their lack of familiarity with computers; they need not worry about having to control the computer in addition to controlling the class; yet they can gradually incorporate CALL materials into their programme of studies by giving students homework tasks using computer programs. Most CALL activities lend themselves to being used in this way, including discussion activities. It is important to remember that self-access does not necessarily mean that learners have to work alone: they can, and often do, choose to work on a program together.

The computer should be located in a 'neutral' place, preferably not the maths department or a science laboratory. The school library is a good place, especially if there is adequate supervision.

This situation is not ideal, however, as the language teacher will face strong competition for the machine from other departments. Much more can be achieved if the computer belongs to the language department, and is available for classroom use.

Given that a large enough screen is available, the easiest way of exploiting one computer is to involve the whole class in a 'frontal' activity. This could be a text reconstruction task, with the teacher controlling the discussion and students taking it in turns to operate the keyboard. Simulations are also possible: the class can be divided into groups, each with a different role, who come to decisions in group discussion, then defend them in whole-class discussion, the final decisions being fed into the machine. Or the teacher may decide to present a new language point using an animated presentation program, then turn the machine off and continue with conventional practice activities: there is no need for the computer to dominate the whole lesson.

Perhaps more satisfactory are activities in which groups of learners take it in turn to use the machine. Such activities require careful preparation, as groups must be kept busy while they are not at the keyboard. A variety of tasks are possible: one is a writing activity using the word-processor, as described on pages 51–52. Another is a simulation. We saw on page 66 that some simulation programs can cater for a number of different 'players' at once: while awaiting their turn, a group can be discussing the results of their last decision, writing them up, or preparing for their next turn. Alternatively, work at the computer can be just one of a variety of options: one group can be working on a question-and-answer program at the keyboard, while the others are doing paper-based exercises or group listening activities. The teacher, meanwhile, is busy giving individual attention where needed.

Several computers per class

Many of our lesson descriptions have assumed the possibility of groups of learners working simultaneously at different computers, and for many purposes this is certainly the best arrangement. The teacher may, of course, sometimes elect to use only one: this may be for pedagogical reasons, for example with certain kinds of simulations, or to minimise complexity if learners and teacher are newcomers to CALL. But by and large, money spent on extra machines is not wasted.

Some thought should be given to the composition of groups for a CALL activity. Certain considerations – the mixture of mother tongues, ability levels, and so on – apply to CALL as to any other groupwork activity, but there are other CALL-specific criteria which should be borne in mind:

1 It is useful to have at least one learner per group who has some familiarity with the computer keyboard. As time goes on, this will be no problem, as students generally have no trouble in picking up rudimentary keyboard skills.

2 Group size is also important. The ideal number is three – one at the keyboard, and one learner on either side. At a pinch, five is all right provided the seating is so arranged that the two outside learners have a clear view of the screen. Four, however, is less desirable, as there is a tendency for the fourth learner, the 'odd man out' furthest from the screen, to feel a little out of things. One way of avoiding this problem is to shuffle the seating arrangement now and again.

3 A final consideration is sex. It is usually the male students in a group who 'already know all about computers', and it is not uncommon for the lone female to get less than a fair crack of the whip. Alternatively, she may, if she has typing skills, receive the 'secretary treatment', her role reduced to a mere interface between the machine and the rest of the group. Whether these situations arise will depend on the individual personalities involved, but if they do, it might be fairer to have single-sex groups.

5 Conclusion

In Part 1 we have tried to show the benefits that computers can bring to language learning. Because the computer is capable of playing so many different roles in and out of class, we believe it to be the most exciting and potentially useful aid so far available to language teachers.

At the same time, we have tried to dispel any mystique surrounding CALL. The computer is just a mechanical device which can be used well or badly. Without careful choice and preparation of materials, careful lesson planning and classroom management, and training of both learners and teachers, the computer is useless. The crucial element, as always, is the teacher.

15

Choosing hardware

1 Introduction

The first task of any school that wishes to embark on CALL is to purchase the necessary equipment, or hardware: the computer, disk drive, monitor (or screen) and printer. The right choice of computer is crucial: although prices have fallen rapidly over the past few years, and are still coming down, a set of several computers plus peripherals still costs a lot of money, and mistakes can be expensive. They are also easy to make. The marketing of computers is a cut-throat business, and salesmen can be very convincing, especially when the buyer knows little about the field. In this chapter, therefore, we look at some important things to bear in mind when choosing hardware in general, and the computer in particular.

Many teachers, of course, will not be able to choose which computer to buy: the choice will have already been made for them, either by a teacher in another school department (often the Maths department), by the head teacher, or, more probably, by the regional or national government. In this case, the problem could simply be one of prising some machines away from the science teachers and obtaining relevant software from whatever national scheme is under way.

The likelihood is, however, that things will not be that simple. National and even regional schemes are often slow at getting off the ground, and the chosen machine may not be suitable for the language teacher's needs, for reasons that we will see below. In this case, the teacher could be faced with the problem of persuading school authorities to part with money for a different machine, or might even decide to buy and use his own.

Whatever the situation, the first time buyer should try to obtain as much information and advice as possible before committing himself. In a rapidly changing field like computing, confident advice is difficult to give, but there are certain important things to look out for in a machine destined for the language classroom.

2 Hardware and software

The key to finding suitable hardware is to look for suitable software. It is an unfortunate fact that software written for one make of computer will almost certainly not work on another: sometimes this is true even of different models made by the same company. And a computer without any programs is about as useful as a record-player without any records. Because programmers tend to write for machines that sell well, the best course is to follow the market and buy a well-known machine, particularly one that is doing well in local schools. Computers already widely used for CALL include various models of the Acorn BBC, the Apple, the Commodore and the Sinclair Spectrum. Others for which the amount of language software is growing include the Amstrad at the cheaper end of the market, and the IBM PC at the pricier end. (See Fig. 15.1.)

It is no coincidence that these are machines that sell well in America or Britain. From the English teacher's point of view they have a definite advantage, in that the software written for them uses *English*, and there is consequently a rich source of programs of all kinds – not just educational programs – that can be exploited in the EFL class. This can present a problem in countries where the school system has universally adopted a locally made machine, however good it may be: the English teacher is unable to tap the wealth of software written for other machines, and can only wait for suitable materials to appear locally, or get on and write it himself.

3 Other considerations   When choosing amongst well-known makes of computer, there are several criteria that should be borne in mind:

- How much does it cost? Prices for a complete system, with monitor and disk drive, range from about £350 to over £2000. Are any discounts available for educational purchases, or for bulk buying? For a teacher buying a machine out of his own pocket, a secondhand machine is a possibility.
- Does the computer have both upper and lower case? Nowadays most do, but some do not.
- Can it produce colour? If so, is the colour limited to graphics, or can it print text in colour as well? There are advantages to be gained by highlighting different words in different colours.
- What is the keyboard like? Try it out with a program for a few minutes. Has it got typewriter-style keys or simply touch-sensitive rubber pads? The latter can be rather irritating.
- Move the keyboard a little from side to side while a program is in memory. Do any of the leads come loose? Remember that learners in groups may prefer to move the keyboard rather than themselves.
- Will the computer produce any extra accents or diacritics that you need for work in foreign languages? If so, can they be accessed easily by the user? Ask for a demonstration.
- How much memory does the computer have? It should have at least 32K, preferably more. Many computers can be expanded with additional memory packs that can be bought at a later date.
- Can the computer support a disk drive, or are you limited to cassettes? Does it have suitable connections for a printer to be attached?

15.1 *Some popular microcomputers.*

Commodore 64

IBM PC

Acorn BBC

Apple IIe

ZX Spectrum

Amstrad

– Look at the user manual. Can you understand it? Many manuals are written in complicated jargon that only experts can understand – and experts don't usually need them.
– Can the computer be serviced locally? Is there an after-sales service? Even if nothing mechanical goes wrong, you will almost certainly need advice on setting the system up. For this reason it is usually better to buy your computer from a specialist dealer than from a department store or discount store. And, unless you can call on skilled technical assistance within the school, you would be well advised to have a service agreement to cover any breakdowns.

Finally, don't confuse the criteria for a computer destined for educational use with those for a business computer. They may have different requirements regarding printer specifications, memory capacity, monitor design and software. The computer in use in your school office may well not be the one you will choose to use with students.

4 Cassette or disk?

The only advantage of using cassettes rather than disks to store programs is that of price. The computer itself will be cheaper without the modifications needed to use disks, disk drives themselves are expensive, and cassette-based programs are usually slightly cheaper than disks.

There are a number of disadvantages:

– Since the volume setting of the cassette recorder is critical, cassette-based programs may not load successfully at the first attempt – a considerable handicap if the class is waiting for their program to load up. This almost never happens with disk-based programs.
– Cassette-based programs take far longer to load than those on disk, a matter of minutes rather than seconds. This, again, can be a problem if something goes wrong and the program is lost. With a disk, it can be almost instantly reloaded.
– If there are several programs on a cassette, accurate records have to be kept of counter numbers; otherwise the computer has to search the cassette for the required program, which can take a long time. Disk-based systems, on the other hand, have 'random access', and can locate a program instantly.
– Some database programs, which require fast searching of the information stored, cannnot be used on cassette-based systems.
– Since disks are easier to protect against illegal copying, and are in any case much less cumbersome to use, some new programs are only being published on disk.

5 Network or stand-alone system?

A decision that will probably be taken by a higher authority than that of an individual teacher is whether to invest in a *network* or in stand-alone machines. In the former case, the computers are linked together (hence 'network') and share expensive peripherals such as a disk drive and a printer. In the latter case, each computer forms an independent unit with its own peripherals. Each system has advantages and disadvantages.

The chief disadvantages of networks are that they require a network manager in order to function efficiently – which can be expensive unless the school already has someone with the necessary expertise – and that some software needs modifying before it can be transmitted over a network.

Their main advantage lies in the simplicity of accessing programs. With a stand-alone system, the teacher either has to provide one disk for each computer, or takes the disk from one to another to load the program, whereas in a network, learners at each machine can all access the same central disk drive by selecting from a simple menu. Networks also offer the possibility of communication between machines, a facility taken advantage of in, for example, the British Council's **Fast Food** simulation.

There is a further advantage to be gained if a school can afford to use a *hard disk* system with a network. A single hard disk has a very large storage capacity – certainly enough for the needs of a sizeable language school – and eliminates altogether the need to manipulate and organise large numbers of floppy disks. A hard disk also allows almost instantaneous loading of programs – a matter of a fraction of a second.

Depending on the number of computers involved, stand-alone systems may initially be more expensive than networks. They are, however, more flexible and less dependent on technical expertise. They have the further advantage that the whole system does not rely on one central machine which might break down.

As both systems have much to be said for them, the best thing for an intending purchaser is to visit schools which have them and see them in action.

6 Integrated unit or separate components

Check whether the monitor, keyboard and disk drive (if you decide on a stand-alone system) form one unit or if they are all separate, connected by cables. The advantage of the single unit is that it is more easily transported from room to room. There are also fewer cables to be tripped over and for students to fiddle with.

Separate units, on the other hand, can be more flexible. If students are working in a group, the separate keyboard can be placed to one side of the monitor, so that the typist does not block the others' view of the screen. Some keyboards are now totally separate from the other parts of the computer, the information being transmitted by infra-red signals. And like stand-alone systems, separate units are less vulnerable to breakdown. If the monitor develops a fault, for example, this need not put the whole system out of action: a television can be brought in as substitute while the monitor is being repaired.

7 Choosing a disk drive

Although there is usually a variety of disk drives available for a given computer, it is usually safest to go for the most commonly used. Take particular care that you do not choose, for example, a 3½″ disk drive if most software for your computer is produced on 5¼″ disks.

Whatever make you choose, you will find both single and dual drives available. The latter have room for two disks, and are particularly useful for copying the contents of one disk onto another. For this reason, it is useful for a school to have at least one dual disk drive. Multiple copies of disks are needed not only for work on several machines at the same time, but in case of damage to the 'master' disk.

For most student uses, single disk drives are adequate, although some programs require two disks: one for the program, the other for data. With a dual drive, the learner will not constantly need to change over disks.

Some computers have more than one format for disks. For example, the Acorn BBC operates with either 40-track disks (which can hold 100K) or 80-track (which hold twice as much), but 80-track disks cannot be used with a 40-track disk drive. Such problems can be avoided by buying switchable drives which can operate on either 40 or 80 tracks. Switchable drives can be either single or dual. They can also be double-sided, accessing both sides of a disk. A double-sided 80-track disk can hold 400K – four times as much as a single-sided 40-track disk – and with blank disks at up to £2 each, such extra storage capacity is very much worth having.

When buying a computer system, make sure that the price you are quoted includes any necessary extras such as cables to link the disk drive to the computer or extra chips needed inside the computer itself.

8 Choosing a monitor

The main choices here will be between a colour or monochrome monitor, or a television. Monitors give a much clearer picture than a television, and this makes them more suitable for close-up work in groups, although a large television will be useful for whole-class work.

As the photographs in Part 1 show, colour can be used to good pedagogical effect in CALL, as well as being more attractive than monochrome, but a colour monitor is likely to be about three times the price of a monochrome screen, depending on whether it has low, medium or high resolution. If a monochrome monitor is chosen, a green or amber screen is often found to be easier on the eyes than a black and white one.

The cheapest option, a black and white television, sometimes causes eye strain when used for prolonged periods.

We should here mention the concern felt by many that computer users may be harmed by radiation emissions from the monitor. While there is no hard evidence for this claim, it is probably best to limit sessions at the keyboard to two or three hours at a time. For those who use computers for long periods, add-on screens are available which cut out glare and static discharge, and protective aprons can be obtained for pregnant women working with monitors.

9 Choosing a printer

The two main types of printer are *dot matrix* and *daisywheel*. We have already looked at the capabilities of dot matrix printers in Chapter 8. A daisywheel printer operates as an automatic typewriter, the letters being on an interchangeable wheel (or daisywheel).

Dot matrix printers are much faster than daisywheels (unless you start paying out large amounts of money), and have the advantage of being able to print in a variety of styles in the same document. Daisywheels can also do this, but the printing has to stop while the wheel is changed for another, thus slowing down the printing process even more.

The main advantage of the daisywheel printer is the 'letter quality' of the print. In the language classroom, however, the convenience, speed and cheapness of the dot matrix printer makes it preferable for most purposes, especially with the coming of 'near letter quality' (NLQ) printers, which produce dot matrix output that is almost indistinguishable from a typed page.

There are, as always, some points to look out for when choosing a dot matrix printer:

– Is it easy to load paper? Some printers have extremely complicated, time-consuming ways of loading continuous stationery.
– Is the printer 'Epson-compatible'? Epson is one of the leading printer firms, and its printer commands have become standard.
– Does the printer have 'true descenders': that is, do the 'tails' of letters like *g* and *j* descend below the other characters? If not, the print looks clumsy, and is awkward to read.
– Can ordinary continuous stationery be used or must special (often expensive) thermal paper be obtained?
– Does it have *tractor feed*, enabling it to use continuous stationery, or do you have to feed it with individual sheets of paper?
– How noisy is it? Noise can be reduced by placing printers on specially designed mats.
– What speed does it print at? A good dot matrix printer will print at 160 characters per second, or at about 40 in near letter quality mode.

10 Conclusion

Before buying any computer equipment, get as much advice as you can. This can be obtained from computer journals, from colleagues, and from schools who are already using CALL. Go to several different shops; ring up mail order firms; go to computer exhibitions; don't be afraid to ask questions. Only in this way will you get a clear idea of the advantages and disadvantages of different models and avoid making disastrous and expensive mistakes.

Above all, remember that even a Rolls Royce will not run without petrol, nor will that super little bargain motor with a missing part whose manufacturers have gone bankrupt.

16

Obtaining and evaluating software

1 Introduction

There are two main ways of obtaining computer programs for language learning: the first is to buy ready-made programs, which may or may not include an authoring component; the second is to write them oneself or have them written, either in BASIC or using an authoring language.

In this chapter we look at both of these possibilities, and list some important points to look out for when evaluating programs, whether homemade or commercially produced. We start by looking at different kinds of commercial software, and their sources.[1]

2 Buying programs

Programs suitable for language-learning purposes are of many kinds, and are therefore available from a variety of sources. Information can be obtained from mainline publishers' catalogues, smaller mail-order software houses, journals, computer and EFL exhibitions, and colleagues who are already using CALL.

Although it may take some time to find out what is available, it is time well spent. All over the world, computer enthusiasts are busily writing programs that have already been written and published: in other words, an enormous amount of time is being spent, not only by language teachers, on reinventing the wheel. Writing a computer program, trying it out with students, incorporating modifications, preparing documentation, is an extremely lengthy process. The program you buy will almost certainly turn out to be cheaper than the program that you write yourself or have written for you.

Here is a summary of the types of available software for language learning, and the places to look for them. The annotated software directory on page 140 and the bibliography on page 149 also contain useful information.

Independent courses

There are a number of packages that claim to be complete courses in themselves, or at least systematic revision/remedial courses. These are usually based on question-and-answer techniques, and include

Apfeldeutsch for German and the **Clef Course** for French.[2] Examples of EFL packages are VIFI: Nathan's **Anglais** and Regent/ALA's **Grammar Mastery Series**. Details of such courses can be found in publishers' catalogues.

Courseware

EFL publishers are beginning to produce programs related to their published courses. Longman's **Quartext**, for example, uses texts from the Strategies and Kernel series, and CUP are publishing software relating to the Cambridge English Course. It is possible, of course, to create similar materials for any course by using authoring programs, but attention should be paid to copyright laws.

Supplementary EFL material

Some of this material, such as Longman's **Screentest for FCE** and OUP's **Reading for English**, is available from the larger EFL publishers. However, much useful material specific to EFL is published by smaller software houses such as Wida Software, Camsoft, ESM and Castle Software. Catalogues are available from these software houses, but it is always useful to keep an eye out for advertisements and reviews in general EFL publications and in specialist CALL journals such as *MUESLI News, Callboard*, the *CALICO Journal* and the *TESOL Newsletter*. TESOL members should note that there is a TESOL CALL Interest Section.

Supplementary material for native speakers

Much supplementary material designed for native speakers of English is relevant to EFL. Examples are **Word Hunt**, **Word Sequencing** and **Sentence Sequencing** by Acornsoft, and **Starspell** by Griffin & George Software. Information can be found in educational software catalogues and educational journals such as the *Times Educational Supplement*.

General purpose software

General programs of relevance to language learning include:
- educational programs such as geography and history simulations
- ESP-related programs such as business and technical simulations and office software
- leisure programs such as Scrabble and chess, and some adventure programs
- Word-processing and database programs.

For this kind of software, it is useful to scan the popular computer magazines which feature software reviews, program listings and copious advertising. Computer manufacturers will also often provide fairly comprehensive lists of recommended software of various kinds.

Authoring programs

Authoring programs crop up in a variety of places, and are always worth looking out for. Listed programs that have an authoring facility are indicated in the software directory on page 140.

3 The problem of piracy

A regrettably common way of obtaining software is piracy, which probably constitutes the greatest single threat to the development of a wide range of well-produced, reasonably priced CALL materials. The problem is simply stated: CALL materials are expensive to develop, and the price charged by a publisher is directly related to the expected sales. If a significant number of sales are lost because of piracy, any of three things may happen:

- The publisher puts the price up. Schools who choose to pirate materials because of a shortage of funds will then become even more reliant on theft as their way of obtaining software.
- The publisher applies sophisticated protection techniques to stop disks being copied. This will also tend to push prices up. More important, teachers will be unable to make the (legal) backup copies they need both for security reasons and in order to use the same program in several machines at the same time. From the teacher's point of view, unprotected software is far more convenient than protected software.
- The publisher simply stops developing and publishing computer software. Several EFL publishers have already done this, and piracy may well have been a major contributory factor.

There is also, of course, the risk of prosecution for any school found using software which they have not paid for. But whether caught or not, software pirates are hindering the development of CALL. Ultimately they are harming their own prospects as well as everyone else's.

4 Programming languages

Although it is possible to survive by relying entirely on commercial CALL packages, new ideas for programs are cropping up all the time, and it is not uncommon for language teachers to learn a programming language and produce their own software for use in class.

A computer program is simply a list of instructions written in a form the computer can understand: that is, in a programming language. There are several different kinds of programming language:

Machine code

The 'natural language' of computers is called *machine code*, which consists of numbers made up only of 0s and 1s. Unfortunately, although machine code is perfectly comprehensible to a computer, it is very different from any of the natural languages spoken by human beings, and machine code programs are therefore very difficult and time-consuming to write. As an aid to programmers, computers are also provided with *assembly language*, which enables the programmer to write his commands using mnemonics instead of long lists of 0s and 1s, but this kind of programming is still immensely complex, and remains the preserve of professional programmers and enthusiastic hobbyists.

BASIC

It is possible, however, to program a computer without knowing anything about 'low level' computer languages like machine code or assembly language. There are nowadays a number of 'high level' computer languages, of which BASIC is the most popular, which are specifically designed to make it easier to talk to the machine. BASIC is full of English-like commands such as PRINT, IF, LET, AND, OR, END and GOTO, and a BASIC program is therefore much easier to write – and read – than its equivalent in machine code.

There is, as always, a price to pay for this convenience. Since computers do not understand BASIC, they are provided with a 'BASIC interpreter' which translates the BASIC program into 0s and 1s as it goes along. This ongoing translation process takes time, and so BASIC is much slower than machine code – and therefore less flexible. Because of this, BASIC is an unsuitable language for programs that rely on speed, such as arcade games with fast-moving graphics, or word-processors. It is, however, quite adequate for many language-learning applications, and most CALL software is written either in BASIC or in other high-level languages such as PASCAL.

Authoring languages

Simple though BASIC may be in comparison with machine code programming, it still carries with it a fairly large learning load – larger than most language teachers would be prepared to contemplate. Authoring languages are an attempt to make programming even simpler, and offer the amateur programmer a set of commands that are less complex than those available in BASIC. In the same way that BASIC is less flexible than machine code programming, so authoring languages are less flexible

	least comprehensible	most flexible
Machine Code/ Assembly Language	3813 A2 0A LDX #10 3815 BD 08 0A .RPT LDA &A08,X 3818 20 E3 FF JSR OSW 381B CA DEX 381C DO F7 BNE RPT 381C 60 RTS	
BASIC	100 PRINTTAB(0,5)Q$ 110 INPUT G$ 120 IF G$ < > A$ THEN 140 130 PRINT''Well done'':GOTO 150 140 PRINT''Bad luck. It was'';A$ 150 END	
Authoring Language (Microtext)	most + Italian + crew/Italian crew]920 Italian + crew]920 passengers]910 Italian + work + on + ship]920 ITALIAN]72 @]806]900	
Authoring Package	Enter question 4: I have . . . three letters today Enter correct answer: written Enter distractor 1: writed	
	most comprehensible	least flexible

16.1 The more flexible the programming language, the more difficult it is to use.

115

than BASIC. And because they frequently stop to load up information from disk, programs written with some authoring languages run more slowly than their BASIC counterparts. Their advantage lies entirely in their simplicity. The most popular authoring languages are **Superpilot** for the Apple and **Microtext** for the Acorn BBC.

Authoring packages

We have already looked at authoring packages in detail in Chapter 6. Strictly speaking, these are not programming *languages* at all, as they merely allow the 'author' to write data for ready-made programs. They do, however, provide the easiest route to materials creation, as the whole process of data entry is conducted entirely in English. The very fact that the programming has already been done, of course, means that authoring packages come very low on the flexibility scale.

There is thus a relationship between the difficulty of a programming language and its flexibility: the easier a language is for the programmer to use, the less flexible it is, as can be seen in Fig. 16.1. Because of the complexity of machine code, the main choice facing the teacher who wants to go beyond authoring programs is between BASIC and an authoring language.

5 Writing computer programs

Newcomers to computer programming are often surprised to find how easy it can be to write a simple program in BASIC. Inspired by this discovery, they proceed to write programs, often based on question-and-answer techniques, which test students' command of grammatical rules, irregular verbs and so on. These early attempts are invariably unsatisfactory, and will usually 'crash' if used by anyone other than the author. There are three major problems, problems unfortunately not restricted to amateur programs, as we will see later in the chapter. These are *robustness, screen design* and *tolerance.*

Robustness

A program will usually work well if the user presses the right keys. In fact, he rarely does. He may press a letter when the program is expecting a number, or he may press the ESCAPE key just to see what happens. Unless the program is robust, what usually happens is that the program crashes: it doesn't know how to respond to the unexpected keypress, so it simply stops working. A vital component of any program is, therefore, *error-trapping*, or protecting the program against misuse.

Screen design

The on-screen presentation of a program is important for three reasons. First, an attractive and elegant program is more enjoyable to use. Second, thoughtful use of screen space, colour and sound can make a program more effective pedagogically: the highlighting of key words is a simple example. Third, and most important, good design can help the user to operate the program: clarity and the provision of adequate on-screen instructions are both design matters, and an experienced programmer will give these a high priority.

CALL programs need to be tolerant when accepting inputs from the learner, if he is not to be discouraged. As an example, let us take a vocabulary question which expects the answer "dog". As far as the computer is concerned, "dog", "DOG", "Dog", "dog   " (with a space at the end) and "a dog" are all different answers, and unless the programmer has anticipated these variations, the computer will only accept the first as being correct. It is, in fact, fairly easy to get the computer to allow for upper/lower case differences, and to strip out superfluous spaces and articles before judging an answer, but such features are rarely found in homemade programs. The reaction of a learner whose "dog   " (with a space) is marked wrong, and who is then told that the answer is "dog", can easily be imagined: because his superfluous space is invisible on screen, the learner sees the two answers as identical.

There is a good deal of difference, then, between a program knocked up in an enthusiastic afternoon with the aid of a BASIC manual, and one that can be confidently given to learners to work with alone. The difference is that the latter obeys what Rex Last has called the Iceberg Principle, which states:

> For every single visible effect in computing, (a) a great deal of work has been going on below the surface; and (b) a titanic design effort has gone into getting it right.[3]

Our intention here is not to discourage teachers from learning BASIC and writing their own programs. On the contrary, some of the best CALL programs currently in use have been written by full-time language teachers, and we would encourage all teachers with access to a computer to attain at least some knowledge of BASIC, if only to be in a better position to evaluate software written by other people. It is important, however, not to try to run before you can walk, and to think hard about robustness, screen design and tolerance before letting learners loose on your latest program. For teachers who do want to learn BASIC, but are not interested in the more scientific and mathematical applications of programming, we recommend Graham Davies's *Talking BASIC* (Cassells, 1985), which deals with exactly the kinds of problems faced by teachers writing language-orientated programs.

Those who would like to program, but who feel that BASIC is perhaps not for them, might feel happier with an authoring language such as Superpilot or Microtext. Most authoring languages have built-in features that take care of robustness and tolerance, though screen design is still very much in the hands of the teacher/author.

Before leaving this topic, we should mention one other possibility which is increasingly popular in Britain and elsewhere: the writing of programs by a team. The team consists of one or more teachers, who write the program specifications and the language content, and one or more professional programmers who write the program itself. The program is then field-tested in class, and modifications are carried out in the light of this practical experience.

6 Evaluating software

Such is the concern over piracy that it is often not possible to obtain computer programs on approval, returning them if unsuitable as with books. In some countries there are educational software centres where teachers can evaluate software at their leisure – for example, the British Council Library in London. Otherwise, evaluation has to be done at exhibitions, software demonstrations, in computer shops or using borrowed programs. Although it is safe to buy some software on recommendation, it is important to evaluate programs whenever possible before purchase. Here is a checklist of points to bear in mind, which is also useful for planning and evaluating your own programs. Not all the criteria will apply to all programs.

Pedagogic considerations

– What is the program designed to teach? Does it have any obvious contribution to make to language learning? (The answer to this question is not always self-evident, and will depend as much on what the teacher decides to do with the program as on what the program 'does' on its own.)
– Are the on-screen instructions clear and concise? Is the language level of the instructions higher than the language level of the program itself?
– Is the program more suitable for whole-class work or self-access? If the latter, what paper back-up materials, if any, are needed?
– If a simulation, does it allow for simultaneous use by a number of different groups?
– Does it develop in the same way every time it is used, or is there a random element? Can learners use it a number of times without losing interest?
– Is there an authoring component? If so, is it easy to operate?
– How accurate is the language? Are there any spelling or grammar errors?
– If a question-and-answer program, does it allow for a variety of appropriate answers?
– Is there a 'help' function, or are learners left in the lurch if they do not understand?
– Are learners able to exit from the program, or are they forced to plough on to the bitter end?
– And finally, will learners enjoy working with it? If not, forget it.

Program design

– Is the program robust? Try pressing a few keys at random, and see what happens. In particular: try the ESCAPE and BREAK (or RESET) keys; type in a word when the program asks for a number; type in a ridiculously long answer; and press RETURN without typing anything.
– Is the program tolerant? Add a space or two at the beginning or end of an answer; enter an answer in a mixture of upper and lower case.
– Are colour and sound used in interesting ways? Are they used too much?
– Are there any graphics? If so, are they relevant to the program?
– If the program is in colour, and you have monochrome monitors, try the program in monochrome: can you see everything clearly?
– Can the sound be switched off – to avoid disturbing other users?

118

- Is the program on one disk or two? It is easier to set the program up if it is all on one disk.
- Does the program load easily? This is especially important if you have a cassette-based system.
- Does the program require any add-ons such as printers or joysticks (see page 133)?
- Finally, can you make back-up copies? If so, how many?

7 Conclusion

Compared with some other fields, there is still a limited amount of software for language learning, and for some machines the choice is narrower still. Good commercial software, therefore, should be bought and cherished. But there is room for good amateur software as well. Writing your own programs can be very enjoyable, and there is a great satisfaction in seeing your program being used successfully by learners. In both cases, however, the emphasis should be on the 'good'.

The most reliable information about programs, both homemade and professional, will probably come from other teachers. It is very useful to set up a 'Software Corner' in an existing language teachers' journal, or a local CALL User Group, so that teachers can exchange information and tips about software they have used. In this way, new ideas can be shared, and the wheel will not need to be reinvented quite so often.

17

Organisation of resources

1 Introduction

Although many schools will initially have only one computer, this is likely to be a short-lived situation. As staff and students become more proficient at using it, and as its potential is realised, more machines are likely to be purchased, and eventually there may be enough computers to justify the creation of a computer room.

This chapter looks at ways of managing CALL resources: setting up hardware, organising software and allocating job responsibilities.

2 One computer in the school

We have suggested that a single computer is best kept in a neutral place such as the school library. If this is not possible, an alternative would be the staffroom, where teachers would have a chance to try out programs and plan lessons. Whatever the location, the computer is best kept on a trolley, so that it can easily be moved to classrooms as and when needed.

A booking form will be needed to ensure that the computer is not double-booked, and the best place for this is probably next to or attached to the computer or monitor. If the machine is monopolised by certain departments, the booking form can be used to allocate time fairly, reserving a certain amount of time for each subject, teacher or class.

Any available software should be copied if possible and the masters kept in a safe place. The copies should be kept with the computer, on the trolley if there is enough space, or on an adjacent shelf.

3 Expanding the system

As the school obtains more computers, the system will have to be expanded. Computers can now be located around the school, but still on trolleys so that they can be moved elsewhere. At least one machine should be available to teachers for lesson preparation, development work, writing with authoring programs and making back-up copies of new programs.

The location of software depends very much on the circumstances. If more than one teacher is likely to need the same program at the same time, the booking system could be expanded to include software; alternatively, sufficient copies of each program could be made to provide one of everything for each machine. It may, however, be possible to designate each computer to a specific group of users, either according to subject area or language level, and in this case, different programs could be allocated to different machines.

4 The computer room

As the number of computers grows, it is necessary to decide whether to continue to locate them at strategic points around the school or whether to set up a computer room. This usually occurs when there are sufficient computers to enable an entire class to use computers in groups – which may be as few as four or five machines.

There are a number of advantages to be gained by keeping all the hardware and software in one room:

– Most CALL activities are more satisfactory when all the learners are using computers at the same time in groups. The teacher is also spared the task of setting up alternative work for groups who are awaiting their turn at the keyboard.
– Having the equipment in one room makes it easier to organise self-access work, provide training for staff and students, and run extra-curricular activities like a computer or word-processing club.
– A computer room allows central storage of both hardware and software. Because things are moved around less, there is less risk of loss or damage.
– It is easier to protect one room against vandals and burglars than it is to protect a number of rooms spread across one or more buildings.

Putting all the machines together in one room can, however, have disadvantages:

– It may prove difficult to remove single machines from a busy computer room for one-computer lessons elsewhere, particularly if they are bolted down for security reasons, and some worthwhile activities may thus be lost.
– If the staffroom machine has been moved into the computer room to make up numbers, teachers may have less access to computers for necessary development work.
– In a large school, sessions in the computer room may not come round often enough. It might be better to continue with a booking system for single machines than to be able to use the computer room only every three weeks or so.

The answer to these problems is to have two or three machines in addition to those in the computer room. These can be kept on trolleys, moved to the staffroom and classes as necessary, and locked in the computer room at night.

5 Organising the computer room

As important as the decision to set up a computer room is the choice of the room itself. A small, poky room with barely enough space for the machines, tables and chairs will not be much appreciated by students or teachers. Ideally, the computer room would be large and airy, with plenty of space between work stations, so that users do not feel hemmed in by the machinery. Space is also needed for storing software, for reference books of various kinds, and, if possible, for armchairs where students not using the computers can sit and browse. And the less the computer room resembles an old-style language laboratory, the better: small details like posters, potted plants and curtains can have a useful psychological effect on nervous or reluctant users, besides making the room a more pleasant place to be. Any carpeting should be of non-static material, as static can damage disks.

The main decisions to be made concern the organisation of hardware and software and the allocation of responsibilities for the computer room.

17.1 Back-to-back computers in Eurocentre, Cambridge.

17.2 Software corner in Bournemouth Eurocentre.

The organisation of hardware will depend to some extent on whether the computers are linked in a network, or whether each computer has its own disk drive and, possibly, printer. The latter will clearly require more space at each work station. If a printer-sharing device is used, the machines will have to be grouped near each other.

To help achieve a non-laboratory look, computers should be arranged not in regular rows but around the walls and in groups in the middle of the room. For those in the middle, semi-circular tables make it easy for groups of learners to cluster round the screen. Space can be saved by arranging some computers back to back (see Fig. 17.1). It is a good idea to put one or two of the machines on trolleys, so that they can be moved around or out of the computer room. Tables, trolleys and chairs should, of course, be the right height for typing, and for keyboard operators, adjustable typists' chairs are helpful.

Use can be made of devices called bridges, which enable the monitor and drives to sit above the keyboard, thus forming an integrated unit. Some bridges have locking covers which act as anti-theft devices.

Provision should also be made for students to make notes as they work through programs. If there is not enough desk space for students to rest notepads, each position can be supplied with clipboards.

Trailing wires should be avoided for safety reasons. It should be possible to install extra sockets round walls and in islands in the centre of rooms. But take care not to overload the circuits.

Care of disks

Disks must be looked after carefully if they are to give good service. The following rules should be observed:

- Always keep disks in their protective envelopes.
- Only use felt-tipped pens to write on labels, and don't press hard. Better still, write on the label before sticking it on the disk.
- Avoid dust, smoke and food particles. Smoking, drinking and eating should be banned in the computer room.
- Do not put anything on top of disks.
- Take care when inserting disks into disk drives.
- Never put disks near magnets or strong magnetic fields such as those generated by monitors, televisions, tape recorders, telephones or transformers.
- Do not bend disks.
- Never touch the exposed recording surfaces.
- Avoid direct sunlight, excessive cold and damp conditions. Temperatures between 10° and 52° Centigrade are suitable.

Storage of disks

In theory disks should be stored in (expensive) purpose-made boxes. In practice, one of the authors and several of her colleagues have stored disks for years in supermarket carrier bags. Many teachers simply keep disks in the cardboard boxes in which they are supplied, labelling boxes according to the level or topic of the programs. Others have tried a more sophisticated system whereby the disk and all accompanying documentation are kept in a folder, the problem being to ensure that the contents are replaced every time the disk is used. Yet another system uses specially designed plastic bags which hang from racks or carousels and which can contain not only disks but also documentation and supplementary material.

One fairly successful way of storing disks is shown in Fig. 17.2. The disks are stored in wooden trays in a kind of chest of drawers. Each tray has a paper lining giving details of the disk, the programs contained on it and loading instructions. Students take the whole tray to the computer. The notice boards above the chests provide display space for publicising new programs and displaying catalogues.

Cataloguing programs

The way in which programs are catalogued will again depend on whether a network or stand-alone system is being used.

With a network, the student can call up a topic 'menu', which leads into various sub-menus, allowing him to choose the program he wants. He might, for example, first select a level, then a language skill, then a program.

With stand-alone systems, the students (or teacher) will have to find the appropriate disk and load the program into each machine. The loading is a simple process, but some thought must be given to a suitable system of cataloguing that will facilitate the selection of programs.

One possibility is to set up a series of levels from elementary to advanced, and list the different programs at each level. Some programs may appear at more than one level. In the case of authoring programs, separate disks can be made for each level so that there would be, for example, an elementary grammar disk, an intermediate grammar disk, and so on. Colour coding can be used to make the distinctions clearer.

The programs at each level can then be sub-classified according to either language skill or content. Thus programs at intermediate level may be classified under skills like Grammar, Reading and Vocabulary, or topics such as Business English or Technical English. The disks are then stored according to level. In Fig. 17.2, each level occupies a vertical row of the chest and is clearly marked both in writing and with the appropriate colour code.

Lists of the materials available at each level should be displayed prominently in the computer room and classrooms, and should be updated regularly.

One alternative to this kind of arrangement would be a card index system, the problem being that it is difficult to reproduce and circulate information held on cards. A very useful way of cataloguing resources, as was suggested in Chapter 12, is to keep all the information on a database. As well as computer programs, the database can deal with books, cassettes, videos and self-access worksheets. This enables printouts to be made listing different resources according to level or topic and the location of each item. A database system not only helps users to select and locate items quickly, but is also easily updated.

Other resources in the computer room

The computer room should provide students with a rich learning environment. In it should be kept not only computers and disks, but also reference and supplementary material that will enable students to link the work done in the computer room with classroom work.

Dictionaries, grammar books and lists of irregular verbs will help with many language skills programs. Glossaries will help students work through simulations with a high vocabulary content. If programs related to coursebooks are used then copies should be available. If extracts from readers have been used with authoring programs, copies should be kept in the computer room.

Students should be encouraged to make full use of these resources by large notices on walls reminding them to consult dictionaries and grammar books, to make a note of unfamiliar vocabulary items, to have another look at the coursebook if they are having problems using a program. Also on notices could be teachers' recommendations for self-access work at different levels: these can be changed regularly as the course progresses.

Another very useful addition is a notebook labelled 'Suggestions, Comments and Faults', in which staff and students can write down their opinions of programs, suggestions for new programs and any faults that might occur with the hardware or software.

Use of the computer room

The computer room can be used in several different ways. Classes might be timetabled to use it on a regular basis, or it might be used entirely for self-access. Alternatively, teachers could book the room when they need it: some teachers may be more enthusiastic about using the computers than others. Much depends on the other resources available in the school, on staffing ratios and on teachers' abilities and preferences.

Staffing ratios will also determine the amount of assistance available to students when the computer room is used for self-access. Some schools might be able to allocate a member of staff to be constantly present to help with technical or pedagogical matters; in others, students may have to cope on their own. In our experience, this is no great problem. Students usually prove to be very resourceful and capable of resolving everyday problems. Just as important, they are, for the most part, responsible, and treat both hardware and software with care and respect.

There are, however, a number of jobs that have to be done by staff, and these have to be clearly allocated.

Jobs in the computer room

The jobs to be done in the computer room will again depend on whether the computers are linked in a network or whether they are stand-alone machines. Jobs common to both systems are the following:

- obtaining and evaluating software
- making back-up copies
- cataloguing software
- publicising new programs
- integrating new material into the computer room together with any necessary documentation and back-up material
- replacing damaged disks and lost files
- updating disks if a new version of a program is issued

- preparing clear instructions on how to operate the computers, and displaying them
- preparing lists of things that might go wrong when operating computers, and the appropriate action to take
- acting as a channel for making additions to authoring programs; typing them or getting them typed; updating catalogues and publicising the additions
- maintaining booking forms
- training and helping staff and students
- buying and formatting blank disks
- checking on paper supplies in printers and buying more paper
- updating staff on new programs (a constant process)
- making suggestions about ways of exploiting programs; preparing sample lesson plans.

Jobs specific to network managers include:

- transferring programs to the central disk
- structuring the central disk in a way that makes program selection easy, through a series of menus
- deleting from the disk at regular intervals programs that are no longer required – a task requiring much tact, since you might be deleting a masterpiece of word-processing or programming that has taken someone months to achieve
- making any necessary changes to new software to make it run on the network.

Some of these tasks can be entrusted to a technician, should the school be lucky enough to have one. Others, such as evaluation, preparing documentation and training, will have to be done by a teacher or teacher-trainer.

It may be necessary to distribute the responsibilities among several people, and it is certainly desirable that more than one person in the school should know how to perform the necessary tasks. What is essential is that the system is maintained and that staff and students' confidence in computer-assisted learning techniques is not undermined by technical failure that could easily be avoided.

6 Conclusion

There is much work involved in setting up and maintaining a well-equipped computer room. The results, however, are well worth the expense and the effort put in by teachers. Problems will inevitably arise, but many can be avoided by careful planning, and as in all things, it is easier to prevent things from getting in a mess than to clear up the mess once it has occurred.

For many schools, the cost in money, human resources and space will rule out a computer room for the next few years. But as we have tried to show, there is much that can be achieved with two or three mobile machines, and the experience thus gained will make it correspondingly easier to organise a computer room in the future.

18

Training teachers and students

1 Introduction

Training language teachers to use computers can be very easy: once they have tried out programs in 'student position', teachers are quick to see the point of the exercise, and usually react with enthusiasm. Those problems that do occur usually arise from teachers' general attitudes towards technology. In Chapter 14 we mentioned some of the negative preconceptions that language teachers commonly have about CALL: worries about the complexity of the machine, a fear of the computer as a rival (instead of an aid), and a general scepticism about the computer's potential in language learning.

Such attitudes towards machines were evident when teachers were trained to use language laboratories and, to a lesser extent, video equipment. Yet the advantages of laboratories and video for language learning are fairly obvious; this is not always the case with computers, which cannot provide speech models and have limited graphic capabilities. Training is needed to demonstrate what their advantages are.

Students do not usually share these reservations about computers. For them, computer-assisted language learning often represents a refreshing change from normal lessons, and they are appreciative of the freedom and individual feedback the machine provides. For teachers it may merely represent an opportunity for their weaknesses and technical incompetence to be displayed openly in front of students. Students may have used computers in other lessons or may have one at home; teachers are less likely to have their own home computer, either through lack of interest or lack of money. At a recent conference of language teachers held in Britain, teachers were asked to raise their hands if they had a computer at home; the proportion proved to be well below the national average.

The attitudes described above are not, of course, typical of all language teachers – or of all students. They are, however, fairly common, and should be carefully borne in mind when deciding on training strategies. A certain amount of scepticism is, in any case, to be welcomed: as we have said elsewhere, an uncritical acceptance of all things electronic will do little to further either CALL or language learning in general.

127

2 Strategies for training teachers

Training programmes for teachers should take into account the points made above and include the following aims:

Aims

- to bolster teachers' confidence in their ability to operate the hardware
- to make them aware of the range of programs available and the pedagogic objectives of such programs
- to enable them to integrate computer-assisted learning techniques into their programme of studies
- to encourage them to view the computer as an aid rather than as a rival
- to make them think creatively about what a program can be used for, not only look at what the program does itself.

Choice of strategies

Strategies adopted will depend on the circumstances of individual schools, the variables being the time available for training, the age, attitudes and abilities of the teachers involved, the number of computers available, the range of software and the range of lessons taught. The following suggestions should be treated as such, a list of hints rather than a series of hard-and-fast rules.

In general, training should be practical rather than theoretical. The Chinese proverb is relevant here:

I hear and I forget; I see and I remember; I do and I understand.

As far as possible, teachers should learn by doing; working through programs themselves rather than just observing; loading programs into the computer themselves rather than just watching the trainer do it.

The first training session

One of the main components of computer-phobia is fear of the keyboard. Many of the present generation of teachers were brought up to use fountain pens rather than ballpoints at school. Future, if not present generations of students will be as confident using a keyboard (or alternative devices such as light pens, mice and touch-sensitive screens) as present-day teachers are using pens. Because of this keyboard-phobia it makes sense to begin the training with a program that does not require users to input large amounts of data via the keyboard. There are many such programs on the market, most of them using the cursor (or arrow) keys to indicate chosen responses from a list displayed on the screen.

It is also important to choose for the first session a program with clear pedagogic objectives; that will load without problems; that has absolutely foolproof, crystal-clear instructions; and that will not crash if teachers press the wrong keys. First impressions are vital and can determine attitudes for a long time in the future.

If at all possible, all the teachers present should work through the program, preferably in groups and using the target language. While they are doing this they can be asked to monitor the language they are using.

After working through the program they can come together to share their reactions. The trainer can try to elicit from them the pedagogic objectives of the program, discuss whether or not they were achieved, deal with any technical problems, underline, if appropriate, the amount of

128

interaction in the target language that was stimulated by the program and generally encourage teachers to talk about the experience.

It is a good idea for the program used during the first session to be an authoring one. Teachers should not necessarily be expected to use the authoring component, but they should understand that the same program framework can be used with a variety of texts or data, thus making the program versatile, and useful at a variety of levels and for a variety of topics. It should, for example, be pointed out that a multiple-choice or gap-fill program can be used for vocabulary reinforcement or grammar practice at various levels, using data taken from general, business or technical English.

Using this experience as a basis for discussion, the trainer can try to elicit from teachers sample lesson scenarios in which such a program could be used. He can then recount his own experiences in using such programs and distribute lesson plans.

The trainer should emphasise that teachers will not suddenly be expected to use a vast range of programs. Fairly low objectives should be set, probably not expecting teachers to use more than one or two programs at first, and only extending their range when they feel quite confident about doing so.

It should also be made clear that, apart from actually throwing it on the floor and jumping up and down on it, there are not many ways of actually damaging a computer. Some teachers have a great fear of breaking machines, and these fears should be set at rest. Teachers should, however, be aware of the guidelines for looking after disks which were described in the last chapter.

Follow-up

As follow-up to this first training session, the trainer can make available to staff further sample lesson plans using the programs they are familiar with (or, later, as they gain confidence, incorporating new programs), and perhaps videos of lessons using these programs.

If staffing ratios allow, he can encourage other members of staff to observe lessons in which the computers are used and to participate in such lessons by team-teaching.

Depending on the time available and on staff willingness to attend, he can then organise further workshops and training sessions to familiarise teachers with a wider range of programs and ideas for CALL lessons.

Further hints on strategies

- Work from the classroom to the computer, not vice versa. For example, ask teachers what data *they* would like to include on authoring programs, thus linking existing classwork with new, computer-assisted techniques. Only later will teachers be able to take a new computer program and integrate it into their programme of studies: they must first work the other way round, on the firm foundation of their classroom experience and the materials they already use. This is why authoring packages are so valuable.
- Teach things in stages, one program at a time, always linking training sessions to the classroom, suggesting and eliciting classroom uses.

- Keep teachers away from computer manuals. With very few exceptions they are written in a variety of English that is incomprehensible even to native speakers.
- Don't teach them anything about the inside workings of computers unless they are genuinely interested. It is not necessary to understand the working of an internal combustion engine in order to drive a car; neither is it necessary to be acquainted with semi-conductors or microchips in order to use a computer.
- Similarly, a knowledge of programming is by no means a prerequisite for using computers. A number of teachers will become interested and will wish to learn how to write programs, and it is true that a knowledge of programming helps teachers to understand what computers can and cannot do. But it is certainly not essential and should follow rather than precede practical sessions on how to use hardware and software.
- Be approachable. Teachers will probably sidle up to you in corners and confess their anxieties. Like the rest of the population, teachers do not relish admitting their shortcomings in public.
- Try to encourage teachers to learn from students – a sore point for some teachers who like to imagine themselves as unchallengeable sources of authority in their classrooms. Computers are great levellers and no respecters of dignity.
- Within the constraints imposed by the last point, try to use enthusiastic students and teachers as multipliers, familiarising others with new programs and sharing tips and techniques.
- Make journals and books freely available to staff. Encourage them to look through software reviews and advertisements to identify programs that might be of use to the school. If they have a stake in them they are more likely to learn to use them.
- Don't give the impression that the use of computers is the only training objective in the school. Include other topics. Stress that computers are not the be-all and end-all of language learning, but simply a very useful aid.
- And if some teachers reject all help and refuse to use computers, do not force them to do so. It is counter-productive to require a teacher to use in class a technique of which he disapproves. His true feelings will show through and the lesson will almost certainly fail.

3 Strategies for training students

Training students to use computers is almost invariably easier than training teachers. There are several reasons for this. First, students merely have to operate the hardware and learn from the software: they do not have to integrate it into lessons. Second, they have often used computers before; if not, they are usually very willing to learn. Third, they tend not to be so critical of the software as do teachers; if they do make comments they tend to be in the form of constructive suggestions.

As with teachers, the strategies used will depend on the age, attitudes and abilities of the students and the type of computer installation used.

The following suggestions may be useful:

- The main emphasis should be on practical training. Students should be able to choose an appropriate program and load it into the computer.
- They should understand how to handle and look after disks.
- They should be encouraged to think about the reasons why they are using computers; to identify the skills that various programs are designed to develop; to realise that they are not merely playing games, but that CALL can be useful as well as enjoyable.
- They should be aware of the importance of linking work done on the computer with work done in class, and should be encouraged to use programs linked to their coursebook, to current grammar topics, to relevant vocabulary or some other appropriate area.
- They should be made aware of the importance of study skills, noting down unfamiliar vocabulary items, consulting dictionaries and grammar books.
- They should realise the importance of communicating about programs in the target language.
- Neither of the authors has had any problems encouraging female as opposed to male students to use the computer. They are generally perfectly happy to work on an equal footing. They do, however, often express a preference for more serious and overtly pedagogic programs, spurning (quite rightly) the often bloodthirsty and aggressive adventure games favoured by males.
- As with teachers, technophobic students should not be obliged to use computers against their will. They will often be happy to watch their colleagues working and may eventually wish to join them. As a last resort they can be given other work to do.

4 Conclusion

Given sufficient time and sympathetic training, the vast majority of language teachers and students will use computers. As with other aspects of language teaching, some teachers will be more enthusiastic and will travel further along the road than others; this is only to be expected. What is important is that no teacher or student should be deterred by fears of technological inadequacy from experimenting with computers.

19

Taking things further

1 Introduction

In Part 1 we looked at a wide variety of computer programs and at different ways of exploiting them in the language classroom. Part 2 has been concerned with the practical problems of introducing CALL into a language programme: selecting hardware and software, organising and maintaining a workable system, and training teachers and students to make effective use of the equipment.

Most of the activities that we have described require only a basic system – a computer, disk drive, screen and, in some cases, a printer – and there are no doubt many other useful applications for this basic system in language learning. Occasionally, however, a CALL activity can be enhanced (or a new activity made possible) by using an extra piece of equipment, or *add-on*. In the chapter on listening skills, for example, we looked at computer-controlled cassette recorders and speech digitisers; we also made a brief mention of interactive video. And in the chapter on databases, we discussed the use of the modem as a means of communicating with the outside world.

As teachers become more familiar with computers, and more confident in their ability to use them, they may wish to experiment with these and other add-ons, either incorporating them into their own programs or buying programs which make use of them. Below we look at a number of different add-ons, and suggest how they might be useful. Some have been around for some time, but have not been extensively used in CALL programs as yet; others are still very much in development.

2 Input devices

There are a number of ways of inputting information into the computer other than by typing at the keyboard.

Light pens

Light pens can be used to draw directly onto the screen, as if with a pen, or to select from a menu or number of choices. An early use of light pens was to select the correct answer in multiple-choice tests. They can also be useful for letter-formation practice: we saw in the chapter on vocabulary how students can use light pens to trace letters on screen. Another possibility would be a giving directions program, in which a street map is displayed on screen, and the learner uses the light pen to trace a route dictated on cassette.

Touch-sensitive screens Touch-sensitive screens are add-on screens that fit over the normal computer monitor: the user simply touches the appropriate part of the screen with a finger. Touch-sensitive screens are expensive, and are used by the American PLATO computer-aided instruction materials. In general, they have the same potential as light pens, but have a tendency to get rather grubby. Touch-sensitive screens are much used in interactive video.

Graphics pads An alternative to the touch-sensitive screen is the graphics pad or graphics tablet, a tray divided into squares that sits beside the computer, and on which you 'write' with an electronic 'pen'. The effect is similar to that obtained by writing on the screen with a light pen. It is, of course, easier to write on the flat surface of the graphics pad than directly onto the vertical screen.

Joysticks Joysticks, which get their name from plane joysticks, are used to steer the cursor around the screen in any direction, and are most often used in arcade games. They can also be used to select from a menu, like light pens. The joystick is used to place the cursor in the right place, and then a button is pressed to make the selection.

Mice Mice have a similar function, and are commonly used in office software. The 'mouse' is a spherical object on wheels that moves the cursor around the screen when rolled in various directions on a desk-top. Mice are often used in conjunction with 'icons', on-screen pictures that represent various options: a word-processor menu, for example, might have pictures of a filing cabinet (for loading and saving files) a wastepaper basket (for deleting files) and a typewriter (for printing files). The mouse is used to move an arrow to the desired icon, which is then chosen by a button-press. Because these pictures use up a lot of computer memory, icons are normally restricted to larger microcomputers.

Concept keyboards Concept keyboards are often used in programs for young learners. A concept keyboard is a flat tray on which different sets of symbols may be written. A maths program for young children might, for example, contain the symbols for the numbers 1 to 50, the child pressing the appropriate number to answer addition and subtraction problems displayed on screen. In a multiple-choice program, it might just contain the letters A to D, and the user would merely have to choose from one of these four letters rather than picking his way through the 70 plus keys on the standard keyboard.

Other applications are possible. For example, the layout shown in Fig. 19.1 contains all the commands necessary to solve the Flash Rogers adventure described in Chapter 10. As well as lightening the typing load, it has the advantage of displaying appropriate articles and prepositions.

GO NORTH	GO SOUTH	GO EAST	GO WEST	GO UP	GO DOWN
SHOOT	TAKE	USE	THROW	UNLOCK	<ENTER>
READ	LOOK AT	GET INTO	LEAVE	JUMP	<DELETE>
KING KONG	SUSIE STARLET	SOME PETROL	THE DOOR	THE KEY	<HELP!>
THE MAP	THE GUN	THE PLANE	SOME WATER	THE PARACHUTE	<EXIT>

19.1 Concept keyboard layout for playing Flash Rogers.

Voice recognition

The ultimate in input devices is, of course, voice recognition, enabling the computer to understand spoken commands with no need at all for a keyboard. Remarkable strides are being made in this direction: the Alvey programme in Edinburgh, for example, is developing a voice-driven word-processor that is already capable of 90 per cent correct recognition of items from a word list of some 5000 items. We are, however, a long way from having similar facilities on microcomputers.

While each of these input devices has its advantages, and all are fun to use, they are not strictly necessary for most purposes, and can be considered as luxuries. The versatility of the traditional keyboard should not be underestimated, nor the ability of learners to master it.

3 Modems

In Chapter 12, we saw how a modem can link a computer, via the phone line, to commercial databases and to microcomputers in other schools that are also equipped with modems. Here are brief descriptions of two projects which further illustrate the potential of the modem for information retrieval and long-distance communication between users.

A series of articles by Marjorie Vai in the magazine *Dowline* seeks to teach young readers to make effective use of the Dow Jones **News/ Retrieval** database in the United States. As well as tasks that require the user to find information via the keyboard about current films, news and sports, the articles also provide the framework for a number of simulations such as investing notional money in stocks and shares (this one lasts for several months as students track their progress), searching for a job and planning a world tour (complete with an appropriate wardrobe for the various weather conditions). Although these tasks are not specifically aimed at EFL or ESP, they are clearly adaptable for language-learning purposes, and could provide ideas for teachers who want to create their own activities.

More ambitious is **NSIST**, which is 'an on-going, world-wide, multi-institution, educational simulation, involving multi-lingual communications, mainframes, telecommunications and satellites....affiliated to the University of Maryland (USA), with European coordination provided by the University of Toulon (France).'[1] Each simulation takes five weeks, and involves twenty university teams, each representing a different country. Starting from a realistic world political scenario, the different teams send word-processed messages to each other via the telephone lines – some 3000 in all, in seven different languages – simulating developments on the international political scene. The simulation is intended to contribute to the study of international relations, languages, and cognitive skills such as working in teams and making group decisions.

While most language-teaching institutions will not have the resources to run a simulation on this scale, smaller 'on-going' simulations could certainly be set up among schools which have microcomputers and modems, on whatever subject is thought to be appropriate.

4 Voice output

We have looked at some of the advantages of using computer-controlled cassette recorders and speech digitisers, in the chapter on listening. Although add-ons like the AECAL have enormous potential in CALL, and are likely to be high on the priority list of schools already using computers, surprisingly little commercial software is so far available, and this is an area ripe for exploitation by programmer-teachers.

One possibility would be a spoken version of **Close-up**:[2] the computer would display a number of news headlines on screen, then start to play a randomly chosen part of one of the relevant news items. The learner's task would be to identify the matching headline as quickly as possible by pressing a key. The quicker the headline was identified, the more points would be awarded. Another would be a simple student-created information service, which allows users to select a topic from an on-screen menu, and then plays the relevant information on the AECAL.

Synthetic speech can also be produced on the computer by the use of a voice synthesis chip. While it is possible to program the computer to give synthetic oral responses to learners using CALL programs, the use of voice synthesis to trot out 'Well done' and 'Bad luck' is little more than a gimmick. Voice synthesis chips are, however, put to good use among students of phonetics at university level. At Leeds University, for example, students experiment with different synthetic voice parameters to gain insight into the phonology of different languages, including English, and it may be that similar experimentation could also be of help to language learners at lower levels.

5 Interactive videodisk

In Chapter 11, we mentioned the use of computer-controlled video recorders in the context of listening comprehension. Interactive video is a comparatively new area – newer even than microcomputer-based CALL – and although there is as yet a dearth of materials for language learning, things are likely to change before long. An increasing number of interactive video packages are becoming available for use in industry and commerce, and some of these will undoubtedly be of relevance and interest to language learners.

A videodisk can store a vast number of high-quality pictures – about 54,000 frames – any of which can be displayed almost instantly on screen, either as moving pictures or stills. It also has two audio tracks, so that, for example, an elementary commentary could be stored on the first track and a more advanced commentary on the second track. The controlling computer in an interactive video program can display the pictures from the disk, normal computer output or a mixture of both.

This combination of text and real moving pictures (instead of the rather crude computer graphics used hitherto) can add much to the standard of presentation, especially of simulation programs. Instead of rudimentary drawings of, for example, an oil rig, the real thing can be displayed on the screen with waves battering it and characters portrayed in real situations. The user can decide what action should be taken at various critical points and can see displayed in full colour and live action sequences the consequences of those decisions.

One interactive video program for EFL that takes advantage of these features is **Danger Mission**,[3] a fast-moving spy adventure set in London. Users have to make contact with fellow spies, identify enemy agents, make their way around London by bus, tube and taxi and get to their final rendezvous without being arrested. Also on the disk are parallel exercises linked to the pedagogic objectives and plot of the adventure. 'Help' functions are available in the form of computer-generated text, videodisk images and the use of the second audio track to vary the level of difficulty of dialogues. (See Fig. 19.2.)

19.2 *Interactive video:*
Danger Mission in action.

Another important feature of videodisks is that they can store large amounts of computer data as well as (or instead of) audio and video material. This gives them great potential as a storage medium for databases. A disk could contain, for example, a complete dictionary of English or a reference grammar. One interesting example of the use of videodisk as database is the **Domesday Project**, which records facts and pictures about every part of Britain on disk. The database, which was created by children in British schools, could form the basis for innumerable classroom projects.

Videodisk players are still expensive, and there are still problems with compatibility – as there are with videotape – but there is no doubt that before long interactive video will become an affordable and potentially very exciting language-learning aid.

6 Conclusion

All of these sophistications of the basic computer system have something to offer, but since money and time are usually limited, choices will have to be made. The main priority for most schools will be to purchase sufficient numbers of computers to make a viable computer room, and to train staff and students to use them. Even if money is available to buy every piece of add-on equipment imaginable, there is little point in doing so if no one has the time to put them to good use. Modems and videodisk players are of little value to anyone if they are simply gathering dust.

We hope that the chapters in this book have been sufficiently informative and stimulating to language teachers to ensure that any computers in their schools will not have time to gather dust. We have tried to emphasise throughout that the computer is a flexible aid that will lend itself to a variety of different purposes; that it is the teacher's servant, not the teacher's master; and above all that it can do nothing, good or bad, on its own. Whether or not it can help our students to learn a language is very much up to us.

Doonesbury   by Garry Trudeau

Notes and references

CHAPTER 1

1 Rather than switching randomly from *he* to *she* we have chosen to use the unmarked form *he* throughout this book. This has no significance other than convenience and we apologise to any reader who feels strongly about this issue. In our experience as many female as male teachers use computers in their classes.

CHAPTER 2

1 The programs described are **Matchmaster, Choicemaster** and **Testmaster**. See GENERAL AUTHORING PACKAGES, page 143.

CHAPTER 3

1 An unpublished program for the Acorn BBC by Christopher Jones. An Apple version is to be found in **Anglais**, page 140.

2 e.g. **Jumbler** (unpublished), **Textbag** (unpublished) and **Close-up** (see page 36). All three are described in Higgins and Johns 1984, pp 55-58.

3 An unpublished program for Acorn BBC by Glyn Jones of Davies's School of English, London.

4 Part of **Anglais**, page 140.

5 By John Higgins. See page 140.

6 One of Graham Davies's **German Routines**, published by Camsoft.

7 See **Sentence Combining** and **Sentence Linking**, page 140.

8 Some other packages are listed under GRAMMAR, page 140.

CHAPTER 4

1 Unless otherwise stated, programs can be found in VOCABULARY, pages 140-141.

2 See LETTER RECOGNITION AND FORMATION, page 140.

3 e.g. **Starspell**, see page 142. 'Flash' programs are fairly simple to write, and many schools use their own in-house programs.

4 Unpublished program by Christopher Jones for Acorn BBC. A similar effect could be achieved with a general jumbling program such as **Word Sequencing**, page 143.

5 One of the programs included in **Matchmaster**, page 143. Also see **Wordpacks**, under VOCABULARY.

6 This program by Chris Harrison for the TRS80, unpublished. Could be set up using **Tic-Tac-Show**, page 144.

7 By Michael Johnson. Published by Wida Software.

8 See **Food, Homes, Exploration** and **Travel**, under SIMULATIONS, pages 144-146.

CHAPTER 5

1 An unpublished maze by Josephine Jones, for Acorn BBC.

2 Unless otherwise stated, programs in this section, plus some maze/branching story programs, can be found in READING, pages 142-143.

3 **Venture Reader,** developed by Jeremy Fox and David Clark at UEA for Apple and Acorn BBC. Acorn programming by Arthur Rope. See page 143.

4 Part of OUP's **Reading for English** package.

5 In an article entitled 'The uses of an analytic generator', details on page 149.

6 The photo is of an unpublished program by Christopher Jones for Acorn BBC. Short sentences are also jumbled by **Sentence Sequencing**, page 142. Tim Johns has produced an (unpublished) suite of Jumbler programs that will do the job described.

7 By John Higgins, published under the name **Pinpoint**, page 142.

8 From an original idea by John Higgins. Published in various versions as **Storyboard, Copywrite, Tell-Tale**.

9 For an interesting article which points out the limitations of such off-screen discussion, see Alison Piper in SYSTEM ed. Higgins, 1986. Our thanks to Glyn Jones for his observation about knowledge-sharing within the group.

10 By Andrew Harrison. See page 146.

CHAPTER 6

1 A number of authoring packages are described under GENERAL AUTHORING PACKAGES, page 143, others under GRAMMAR, READING, WRITING and VOCABULARY.

2 One of the ZX81 **Wordpacks**, see page 141.

3 For **Quartext**, see page 142.

4 For **Vocab**, see page 141.

CHAPTER 7

1 An example of such a program is included in Heinemann's **Travel** package, see page 146. For other punctuation programs, see page 143.

2 Further information about printers can be found in Chapter 8, pages 58-59, and in Chapter 15, pages 110-111.

3 A number of word-processing programs and spelling checkers can be found in WRITING, pages 143-144. The program described in this chapter is **Wordwise Plus** for the Acorn BBC.

4 Our thanks go to David Eastment of Bell College, Saffron Walden, for many of the ideas in this section. See also Alison Piper's 'Computers and the Literacy of the Foreign Language Learner: a report on EFL Learners using the word-processor to develop writing skills' in University of East Anglia's *Papers in Applied Linguistics Spring 1986* for interesting ideas on training EFL students to use word-processors.

5 *Mindstorms* by Seymour Papert (Harvester Press 1980), page 30.

CHAPTER 8

1 Unless otherwise stated, software can be found under WRITING, page 144.

2 We are grateful to Linda Ferreira, Susan Sklar and Annalee Kagen for this use of **Tic-Tac-Show**.

3 A number of such programs are listed under READING, pages 142-143.

4 Commercial databases are discussed further in Chapter 12.

5 Bell College, Saffron Walden. The program – **Belltext** – was devised by David Eastment.

6 The idea that students' work should be 'published' comes from Bright and McGregor 1972, and is quoted in Higgins and Johns 1984, page 84.

7 **Dialog-Crit** is an unpublished program by Burckhardt Leuscher.

8 The *haiku* are the product of an unpublished program by Christopher Jones for Acorn BBC. The sonnet is a product of **Poetic Pam**, an unpublished program for the Apple by Willis Edmondson of the University of Hamburg.

CHAPTER 9

1 A number of simulations are listed under SIMULATIONS, pages 144-146.

2 We are indebted to Glyn Jones for this way of exploiting **Yellow River Kingdom**. A more detailed account can be found in his article 'The Kingdom Experiment' in SYSTEM ed. Higgins, May 1986.

3 **Bleeper** is an unpublished program by John Higgins for the Spectrum.

4 For some useful ideas on using simulations with only one machine, see Michael Carrier's teacher's notes in documentation for **Decision-Taker**, details page 144.

5 *Mindstorms* by Seymour Papert (Harvester Press 1980), pages 19-21 and passim.

CHAPTER 10

1 Programs mentioned in this chapter are listed under ADVENTURES, page 146.

2 An unpublished program for Apple and Acorn BBC, designed by students of Les Ateliers, Paris, and programmed by Christopher Jones.

3 This imaginative use of **Mystery House** was described by Dr Baltra at TESOL 1984, Houston.

CHAPTER 11

1 For **Speak 'n' Spell**, see under SPELLING, page 142. Other programs in this chapter are listed under LISTENING, page 146.

2 One such system is **Supertalker**, produced by Mountain Hardware.

3 **Visispeech** is obtainable from Jessop Acoustics Ltd, Unit 5, 7 Long Street, London E2 8HN.

4 An unpublished program for Acorn BBC by Glyn Jones, used as a prototype for the Eurocentre videodisk program of the same name.

5 **Dictation** is one of three options in the packages **Back Home**, **Micro Stories** and **Micro Verse**.

6 The project is produced by Eurocentres and financed by the Migros Corporation of Switzerland. New Media Productions and Creative Bytes were used as consultants for the creation of the videodisk and the writing of the computer programs respectively.

CHAPTER 12

1 For a list of database programs, see DATABASES. page 147.

2 This (imaginary) project could be conducted with an inexpensive database such as **Masterfile**, see page 147.

3 Our thanks go to Malachy Mulholland of The Bell School, Cambridge, for this account.

4 A database of this kind has been set up by Michael Carrier at Eurocentre, Cambridge.

CHAPTER 13

1 Unless otherwise stated, programs in this chapter are listed under GRAMMAR, page 140.

2 An unpublished program for the Spectrum by Martin Phillips of the British Council.

3 **Loan** and **Apologies** are unpublished programs by Tim Johns.

4 An unpublished program for the ZX81 by Stephen Pulman.

CHAPTER 16

1 The addresses of organisations mentioned in this chapter can be found in the list of useful addresses, see pages 147-148.

2 **Apfeldeutsch** is published by Wida Software for the Apple. The **Clef Course** is published by Gessler, New York, for Commodore Pet, Commodore 64 and IBM PC.

3 *Language Teaching and the Microcomputer*, page 37. See page 149.

CHAPTER 19

1 Information about NSIST is available from David Crookall, Université de Toulon, Avenue de l'Université, 83130 La Garde, France.

2 See Chapter 5, page 36.

3 See also Chapter 11 note 6, page 139.

Software directory

The following is a selection of programs that will be of interest to the language teacher and learner. It does not claim to be a comprehensive list of CALL software. The categories correspond as nearly as possible to those in Chapters 2-19, and where relevant reference is made back to the text. Although the list is dominated by programs written for English many of the authoring programs are used for other languages. We aim to keep this list as up to date as possible, and would welcome all suggested additions and amendments. Whilst every attempt has been made to ensure that the information is correct at the time of going to press, the Publishers cannot accept responsibility for any errors or omissions.

GRAMMAR

A/an (not published; Spectrum version listed in Higgins and Johns 1984) Students enter any noun phrase and the computer selects the correct form of the indefinite article.

Anglais (Longman/VIFI Nathan; Apple) Self-study grammar exercises and games for French learners of English. 15 units, each with 8 activities, on 5 disks + audio cassettes.

Animals (versions for almost all computers in the public domain). The student thinks of an animal and the computer tries to guess which animal it is by asking a series of yes/no questions. The student builds up a database by teaching the computer the names of new animals and relevant questions.

Assistant Series (MicroTac Software; PC) Memory-resident translation and grammar aids. While using word-processors or other application users can get word for word translations or verb form information, etc.

AUTHORING PROGRAMS See GENERAL AUTHORING PROGRAMS, below, for fill-in, multiple-choice and matching authoring programs suitable for grammar practice.

Bon Accord (Wida Software; Acorn BBC) An advanced level translation trainer for learners of French. Draws upon database of students' responses over ten years.

Call for English (Eurocentres Learning Service, IBM PC) A subscription service for disks of text-based comprehension multi-activity exercises created with the Wida/Eurocentres authoring packages. Three disks a year.

Clef (Gessler, IBM PC) A series of lessons and exercises for beginners and intermediate learners of French. Good discreet response analysis routines.

Dragon Files (Camsoft; IBM PC, RM Nimbus, Archimedes) Three sets of 31 files for use with *Fun With Texts* for French learners from beginners to GCSE standard.

English on Call (McGraw-Hill, Apple) General English course at three levels (Beginner, Intermediate, Advanced). Practises conversational English, reinforces basic language skills and concepts, reviews grammar points.

Eurocentres Library Disks (Eurocentres Learning Service, IBM PC). A series of dedicated packages devoted to particular language points and topics, created with the Eurocentres/Wida authoring programs, available either on subscription or for sale.

First Fifty Phrasal Verbs (Independent Software Lucerne; IBM PC) Simple program working over English verbs with four levels of difficulty and a teacher analysis program.

Grammar Examiner (DesignWare; Apple; Commodore 64; IBM PC) A grammar skills game in which players climb from cub reporter to editor-in-chief. Students roll dice and have to answer a grammar question or edit a paragraph. Authoring facility.

Grammatik IV (Reference Software, IBM PC) A writing aid. Helps proof-read work done on word-processor, searching for errors in grammar, style, usage and spelling, highlights possible problems and suggests solutions.

John and Mary (not published; listing for Spectrum version given in Higgins and Johns 1984) Described on page 93-95.

Photofit (not published; listing for Spectrum version given in Higgins and Johns 1984) Described on page 17.

Practical Grammar Series (Intellectual Software; Apple, IBM PC, Macintosh). Three disks each with 200 grammar exercises, automatic scoring, immediate feedback. Each wrong answer branches to an explanation.

Screentest for Elementary, First Certificate, Proficiency (Longman; Acorn BBC; Apple; IBM PC) Practice for three levels of the Cambridge English Examinations. Exercises on space filling, sentence transformation, word formation, sentence completion, dialogue building. Fill-in and multiple choice options.

S-Ending (Not published; described in Higgins and Johns 1984) The computer provides suitable s-endings for any real or hypothetical noun or verb.

Tree of Knowledge (Acornsoft; Acorn BBC) More flexible version of **Animals**.

Tuco (Gessler; IBM PC) A five-disk topic-based program working up from Beginner's German grammar with many exercises.

LETTER RECOGNITION AND FORMATION

Bouncy Bee Learns Letters (IBM; IBM PC) A playful animated bee guides young children through a series of lessons and games designed to introduce and reinforce letter recognition skills and help improve reading readiness.

Happy Letters (Bourne Educational; Acorn BBC, Amstrad 464) Animated letter-matching game for young children with various levels and speeds.

Happy Writing (Bourne Educational; Acorn BBC, Amstrad 464) Draws letters, numbers or words, showing where to start, which directions to take and where to end. Upper and lower case, adjustable speed and sound levels; variable wordlist.

Letterhunt (CUP; Acorn BBC, Apple) Letter discrimination arcade game. Authoring facility.

Letters (Chalksoft, Acorn BBC) Five programs which show young learners how to form letters correctly by copying what is presented on the screen. The programs group the letters in 'families'.

Reversals (Chalksoft, Acorn BBC) Helps students who have problems writing b for d, p for q, etc.

Sesame Street Letter-go-Round (CBS; Atari, Commodore). Letter recognition and simple spelling game.

VOCABULARY

Alphagame See **Vocab**, below and pages 24, 25.

Anagrams See **Vocab**, below and page 25.

Code Breaker (CUP; Acorn BBC, Apple, IBM PC) The user decodes sentences which have been encoded by simple letter substitution. Authoring facility.

Crossword Challenge (Wida Software; Acorn BBC; Apple) Thirty EFL crossword puzzles at Longman Structural Readers stages 5 and 6. Two-player option.

Crossword Magic (Mindscape; Apple, Atari, Commodore, IBM) Authoring program for generating and printing crosswords.

Crossword Master (Wida Software; Acorn BBC; Apple) Crossword authoring program. User can create, save and solve crosswords on-screen. Includes two-player competitive solving mode.

Enigma See **Fun With Texts** under GENERAL AUTHORING PROGRAMS.

Facemaker (Applied Systems Knowledge; Acorn BBC; Commodore 64) Students think of the face of a person they all know and try to reconstruct it, prompted by simple questions from the computer.

Helter Skelter (Wida Software; Acorn BBC) A word classification authoring package featuring three student activities — **Helter Skelter, Odd Man Out** and **Snap-it**. See pages 29, 30.

Linkword (Acornsoft; Acorn BBC) Vocabulary development by 'pun analogy' with the learner's mother tongue. See page 24.

Mindword See **Vocab** below and page 25.

Jeu de Ménages/Umziehen (CUP; Acorn BBC) A graphics program in which learners of French or German tell the computer to place various items of furniture in the correct rooms of a house.

Pathwords (CBS Software; Apple; Atari; Commodore and IBM PC) Students link together adjacent letters trying to create the longest possible words. Timekeeping function.

Pelmanism (or Memory) See **Matchmaster** under GENERAL AUTHORING PROGRAMS.

Prediction See **Fun With Texts** under GENERAL AUTHORING PROGRAMS.

Quelle Tête/Kopfjäger (CUP; Acorn BBC) Learners of French or German build up a face on screen by giving instructions to the computer.

Rambler (Palmsoft; IBM PC) Learners have to form as many words as they can from the given word. There is no time limit. (See also **Word Hunt** below).

Scrabble (Leisure Genius; Accorn BBC, Apple, IBM PC) On-screen version of the board game. Up to 4 players, including the computer, who plays a mean game.

Scrambler See **Fun With Texts** under GENERAL AUTHORING PROGRAMS.

Skullman See **Vocab** below and page 25.

Textsalad See **Fun With Texts** under GENERAL AUTHORING PROGRAMS.

Vocab (Wida Software; Acorn BBC, IBM PC *with Eurocentres*) an authoring program with six different activities. The teacher enters and saves a list of words, each with a gapped context sentence. The learner chooses from six activities: **Word Order, Skullman, Mindword, Alphagame, Anagrams, Which Word?** See pages 24, 25.

Which Word? See **Vocab,** above.

Word Attack! (Davidson and Associates; Apple, IBM PC, Commodore 64) A word display gives meanings and sample sentences for adjectives, nouns and verbs in six categories.

Word Games (MECC; Atari, Commodore 64, Radio Shack 111/4) Three word games to help with visual recall, logical guessing and word association.

Word Hunt (Acornsoft; Acorn BBC) Students have to form as many words as they can from the given word. A time limit is set at the end of which the computer lists all possible words (See page 28 and **Rambler** above).

Wordspin (not published; Spectrum version listed in Higgins and Johns 1984) Described on page 22.

Wordstore (Wida Software; Acorn BBC, Apple; IBM PC *with Eurocentres*) 'Living dictionary' student database program. See pages 27, 28.

Words, Words, Words (Acornsoft; Acorn BBC) Very simple illustrated vocabulary exercises. Students see object and have to type word in. Ideal for beginners.

SPELLING

Gapmaster See under GENERAL AUTHORING PROGRAMS.

Master Spell (MECC; Apple) Can be used by up to 12 students. List kept of all misspelt words that can be used to generate review lessons. Authoring facility.

Speak 'n' Spell (Texas Instruments) An educational toy with a voice chip: the user hears a word in synthesized speech and is asked to spell it on a keyboard.

Spell It! (Davidson and Associates; Apple, IBM PC) Gives spelling rules and 1,000 of the most commonly misspelt words. Four learning activities including an arcade game. Authoring facility.

Spelling Volumes 1 and 2 (MECC; Apple) Practice in spelling over 1,000 words.

Spelling Week by Week (Chalksoft; Acorn BBC) Almost 3,000 words, presented in 23 weekly lessons. Keeps up to 40 student records. Adopts the look, say, cover, write, check approach. Printer facility.

Starspell (Griffin and George; Acorn BBC) Flashcard program which presents a word then asks the student to type it.

READING

AUTHORING PROGRAMS See GENERAL AUTHORING PACKAGES, below, for fill-in and multiple-choice authoring programs suitable for reading comprehension. Other authoring packages in this section.

Cambridge First Certificate Examination Practice Packs A & B (CUP, Christopher Jones with UCLES; Acorn BBC, IBM PC) Multi-activity pack of exercises closely modelled on past FCE papers.

Class Reader 1: Outcome (Cambridge Language Arts; Acorn BBC) A total text deletion program. Users reconstruct letter by letter, word by word. Punctuation deletion option.

Class Reader 2: Yarns (Cambridge Language Arts; Acorn BBC) Branching story program. The demo stories can be extended and new stories created, which can subsequently be used with any of the **Reader** range.

Class Reader 3: Order, Order (Cambridge Language Arts; Acorn BBC) Jumbles letters in words, words in phrases or sentences, or sentences in paragraphs, for the user to unscramble.

Also jumbles lists (dates, alphabetical, etc.). Jumbled texts can be printed out as worksheets.

Clozemaster (Wida Software; Acorn BBC, Apple II, Macintosh) Authoring program for producing cloze exercises up to 50 screen-lines long. Users choose their own deletion rate (every 5th-15th word). Help and cheat features. Printer facility. See page 37.

Double-Up (Research Design Associates; Apple, IBM PC) Authoring program. Learners see jumbled sentence and unscramble it by selecting two words which they think are neighbours.

Gapkit (Camsoft; Acorn BBC; RM Nimbus, IBM PC, Archimedes) Gap-filling authoring package. Gaps can be whole words, parts of words, groups of words. Printer facility. See page 36.

Gapmaster (Wida Software; Acorn BBC, Macintosh, IBM PC *with Eurocentres*) Gap-filling authoring package allowing alternative correct answers; spelling guide. Users can scroll text and select gaps in any order. Numerous help features. Full word-processing text entry.

Missing Links (Sunburst; Apple, Atari, IBM PC) A literary passage appears with letters or words missing. Nine difficulty levels. Authoring facility.

Pinpoint (Wida Software; Acorn BBC, Macintosh, IBM PC *with Eurocentres*) Authoring package. Students guess the titles of gradually revealed texts. Develops inferential reading.

Puzzler (Sunburst; Apple) Students use the strategies of predicting, confirming and integrating to solve each mystery story puzzle.

Quartext (Longman; Acorn BBC, Apple, IBM PC) A collection of four computer games; **Hopscotch** (a cloze variant); **Hide and See** (recreate the whole text word by word); **Tell-tale** (**Storyboard** variant); **Cheat** (**Storyboard** in competition with the computer: can you catch it 'cheating'?) Authoring facility. See page 45.

Reading for English (OUP; IBM PC) A series of reading passages at different levels. Sets of texts with a variety of exercises, including comprehension questions, cloze, sentence building and word study.

Screentest See GRAMMAR

Sentence Sequencing (Acornsoft; Acorn BBC) Students have to arrange sentences to form a paragraph. Authoring facility.

Sequitur (Research Design Associates; Apple, IBM PC) Authoring program. Learners see and rearrange parts of text with sentences jumbled.

Softmill (Softmill of Finland; IBM PC) A series of text-reconstruction and gap-filling programs (**Easymill, Fillmill, Oddmill** and others) containing English dedicated texts and look-up dictionaries in French, German, Spanish or Finnish.

Speedread (Wida Software; Acorn BBC) An authoring program which displays the chosen text for a certain length of time (any of nine speeds). Reading is followed by multiple-choice questions. Also has an untimed reading option. See pages 34-35.

Speed Reader (Davidson and Associates; Apple, Macintosh, IBM PC) As **Speedread** above, but for different computers. Needs BASIC to run.

Story Tree (Scholastic; Apple) Enables students to read and write branching stories.

Storyboard (Wida Software; Acorn BBC, Apple, Macintosh, IBM PC *with Eurocentres*) Authoring program in which a text

typed in (and saved) by the teacher is replaced by blobs and punctuation marks. Students reconstruct it by guessing words, prefixes or suffixes. Various help features. Printer facility. See pages 37-40, 45.

Storywriter (ESM; Acorn BBC) Two programs, **Storymaker** and **Storyreader**, allow users to write and read branching stories.

Varietext (British Council Software Series, CUP; Acorn BBC, Apple, IBM PC) Text reconstruction program. The user chooses between alternative words and phrases. Authoring facility.

Word Sequencing (Acornsoft; Acorn BBC) Students have to arrange words to form a sentence. Authoring facility.

KEYBOARD SKILLS

Typing Tutor (Context Computing; Acorn BBC) Self-instructional typing tutor.

Vu-Type (BBC/Pitman; Acorn BBC) Students work at their own pace, no need to look at a book, drills and exercises for each finger, reports on speed and accuracy, varied screen colour combinations and choice of sound effects.

Master Type (Scarborough Systems Inc; Apple) Original typing tutor which takes the form of a space arcade game.

PUNCTUATION

Mark-up (Research Design Associates; Apple, IBM PC) An authoring program in which teachers enter text and the program strips out the punctuation and makes it all capitals. Students have to restore the correct version.

Puncman 1 and 2 (Chalksoft Ltd; Acorn BBC) Two programs which ask students to restore missing punctuation. Each program contains several different sentences which form a short story. Deals with full stops, capitals, commas and question marks.

Puncman 3 and 4 (Chalksoft Ltd; Acorn BBC) Like Puncman 1 and 2 but with more difficult punctuation such as speech marks and exclamation marks.

AUTHORING LANGUAGES

Calis (Duke University; IBM PC) Halfway between authoring language (where the authors have to learn an authoring code) and an authoring program (where they don't), **Calis** is a versatile, general purpose tool allowing flexible formats, sophisticated answer processing and the importation of tutorial windows.

Hypertext (IBM PC, Macintosh and other computers) Authoring systems for creating interrelated pages of text, graphics and exercises. Is often used as the inter-active vehicle for controlling devices such as laserdisks, compact disk players. On everyone's lips in the late 1980s.

Microtext (Acornsoft; Acorn BBC, Apple, IBM PC) General-purpose programming package. The user designs a series of frames which can contain text or graphics and control external devices.

Superpilot (Apple Inc; Apple) General-purpose programming language.

GENERAL AUTHORING PACKAGES

More specific authoring packages are listed in relevant sections.

Author (ESM; Acorn BBC) Authoring package for creating quizzes, branching stories, adventures, teletext information systems, etc.

Autotutor (DMA Computers/, Trinity College, Dublin; Acorn BBC, IBM PC) An authoring package which enables the teacher to link a micro with a VHS videocassette recorder to create interactive video exercises.

Brainlearn (Studentlitteratur; IBM PC) Authoring system for CALL. Includes some ready-made exercises in English and French.

Choicemaster (Wida Software; Acorn BBC, Apple, Macintosh, IBM PC *with Eurocentres)* Authoring program for writing multiple choice tests. Random/linear and error messages option. Choice of tutorial mode (with immediate feedback) or text mode (with feedback delayed till the end of the test). Also available for French, German, Spanish, Italian and Welsh.

Comet (Wolfram Burghardt, Dept of Modern Languages, University of Western Ontario, London, Ontario, Canada, N6A 3K7; Commodore 4032; Commodore 8032) General-purpose CALL authoring package.

Fun with Texts (Camsoft; Acorn BBC, IBM PC, Nimbus, Archimedes) A multi-activity, mainly text-reconstruction program including **Copywrite** (a variant on **Storyboard**), **Clozewrite, Enigma** (a letter-substitution decoding game), **Scrambler** (in which the letters in each word have been jumbled), **Prediction** (in which the learner picks what word comes next in a text from a set of choices) and **Textsalad** (a re-ordering exercise).

Guide (Owl International and Guide Distribution; PC and Macintosh) A hypertext/hypercard-based system for computer-based instruction incorporating text, graphics, audio and video components.

MacLang (Gessler Publishing; Macintosh) A multi-activity authoring tool allowing exercise creation in a variety of European fonts including Romanian but also Cyrillic.

Matchmaster (Wida Software; Acorn BBC, Macintosh, IBM PC *with Eurocentres)* Authoring program for creating matching pairs exercises. English, French, German, Italian, Spanish and Welsh versions available. Uses same data for generating **Pelmanism** (Memory) game and **Language Snap.**

Question Mark (Question Mark Computing; IBM PC) A flexible testing program including extensive performance report generating facilities. Teachers can switch between question types within the same exercise – multiple choice, how many are correct, fill-in-the-gap, type in the answer – and many more. Graphics module also available.

Study Guide (MECC; Apple) Can be used to create multiple choice, true-false, matching or completing items. Printer facility.

Teacher Utilities 2,3,4 (MECC; Apple) Authoring package for multiple-choice exercises, hangman, word unscrambling, spelling memorization and spelling recognition. Printer facility.

Teaching Assistant (MECC; Apple; IBM PC) Create, edit and store sets of question and answer exercises. Printer facility. Recording of students' scores. Also available in French and Spanish.

Testmaster (Wida Software; Acorn BBC, Macintosh, IBM PC *with Eurocentres)* General question-and-answer authoring package. Writer program has word-processing text entry. Alternative answer permutations allowed for. Extensive help features including spelling checker.

Text Tanglers (RDA; IBM PC) Various text reconstruction activities based upon texts written by teachers using standard word processing packages.

WORD PROCESSING

The selection below is of packages thought to be especially suitable for educational work, but many of the standard word-processors such as Microsoft Word, Word Perfect, etc. will do the job equally well.

Allwrite (ILECC, Nimbus) Simple word-processor for work with European but also Gujurati, Punjabi and other Asian languages.

Bank Street Writer (Scholastic; Apple) Simple word-processing package designed for use in schools.

Edword2 (Clwyd Technics Ltd; Acorn BBC) Educational word-processing package. Aims to teach word-processing and includes French and German characters.

Folio (Tedimen Software; Acorn BBC) Cheap, large-letter word processor for young children. Includes a number of attractive fonts and foreign character sets.

Magic Slate (Sunburst Software; Apple) User-friendly word-processing package designed for a variety of age-levels.

Milliken Word Processor (Milliken; Apple) Very easy to use. Icon-driven. Also has **Pre-Writing and Post-Writing** programs (see under WRITING section below).

PFSWRITE (Scholastic; Apple) Easy-to-use word processor; compatible with **PFSFILE** and **PFSREPORT.**

Processing Words (MECC; Apple; IBM PC) Students enter, edit and format text material. Using a simple electronic mail program, word processing concepts are applied to electronic form letters and mass mailings.

Simply Write (Simple Software Ltd; Commodore Pet; Commodore 64) Easy to use word-processor.

View (Acornsoft; Acorn BBC) Flexible word-processing program for the Acorn BBC and Master micros.

Write On (Arnold-Wheaton; Acorn BBC) Elementary word processing and sentence building.

WRITING

Add-Verse (Cambridge Language Arts Software; Acorn BBC) A program for creating, storing and presenting pages of animated or still shape poems, pictures, diagrams or prose text.

BRANCHING STORIES See READING, above, for branching story programs with authoring components: a useful purpose for creative student writing.

Class Writer (Cambridge Language Arts Software; Acorn BBC) Enables the typing in of pages of text and graphics. Once stored these 'electronic pages' can be read on screen, printed out or used with any **Class Reader** program. Compatible with **Wordwise.**

Deadline (British Council/Cambridge University Press; Acorn BBC, Apple, IBM PC) Students have to work together to produce a guidebook for the area in which they live.

Letter Writer (Leading Edge; IBM PC) A tutorial on the form of writing English business letters.

Post-Writing (Milliken; Apple) A package consisting of two spelling checker disks, two mechanics checker disks (checking on sentence length, commas with subordinating conjunctions, etc.) and a proof-reader disk that enables the teacher to add comments.

Pre-Writing (Milliken; Apple) Consists of **Brainstorming, Branching** and **Nutshelling** programs to encourage students to organize their writing. Works with the **Milliken Word Processor.**

Proteus (Research Design Associates, Apple, IBM PC) An ideas organiser asking a series of questions (Who, why, where, how, when? etc.) about a topic or project. The answers are then fed into any word processor for polishing.

Storyboard This and other authoring programs in the READING section, above, are suitable vehicles for student writing. See pages 37-40, 45.

Storywriter (ESM; Acorn BBC) Enables learners to create and print out branching stories. Up to 50 pages can be written in each story. Reading age of each story is calculated.

Thinktank (Living Videotext; Apple, Macintosh; IBM PC) Useful for brainstorming activities, outlining and developing ideas, keeping records.

Tic-Tac Show (Scholastic; Apple) On-screen version of American noughts and crosses quiz show. The authoring facility is a suitable vehicle for student writing.

SIMULATIONS

America Coast to Coast (CBS Software; Apple; Commodore and IBM PC) Students improve their knowledge of US geography and history by travelling to each of the 50 states and surveying names, capitals, sizes, mottos and selected industries.

Business Advantage (Business Week/Brøderbund, 1988, IBM PC) A real-life business simulation in which the player has to run Chrysler Corporation in a survival battle against General Motors.

Business Games (Acornsoft; Acorn BBC) Contains **Stokmar** and **Telemar** q.v.

Chain Gang (CUP; Acorn BBC) Industrial relations simulations for up to five teams of management and workers. Includes worksheet and other paper materials.

Current Account Package (Interface Educational; Acorn BBC) Banking simulation. Customers can pay in money, write cheques, use cash card facilities, make credit card payments, standing orders, direct debits, etc.

Decision Taker (Longman; Acorn BBC) Students have to allocate labour to different tasks on an industrial production line.

Discovering the Electronic Office (McGraw Hill; Acorn BBC) The use of information technology in a travel agent's airline booking system. Uses role-playing techniques. Topics include communications, map-reading, composing letters, typing correspondence.

Dream House (CBS Software; Apple; Atari; Commodore; IBM PC) Students create homes, designing exteriors and decorating and furnishing rooms.

Estate Agent (Longman; Acorn BBC) Students run an estate agent's office.

Exploration (Heinemann Computers in Education; Acorn BBC) Includes programs on **Tomb Adventurer, Star Gazer, Mapping Skills, Spelling/Word Finder.**

Faisons des Achats (Wida Software; Acorn BBC) Going shopping in French.

Farm (Primary Programs Ltd; Acorn BBC) Students have to manage a five field arable farm for a year, making decisions about what crops to plant, when to fertilise, etc.

Fast Food (British Council/Cambridge University Press; Acorn BBC, Apple, IBM PC) Students run a fast food stall at an exhibition, taking into consideration the weather, number of visitors the previous year, etc.

Flight Path (Storm Software; Acorn BBC; Commodore 64) Simulates running an airline. Involves choice of aircraft,

stopovers, weather, etc. A balance sheet is shown for passenger revenue, aircraft hiring cost, landing, fuel and recovery charges.

Food (Heinemann; Acorn BBC, RML 480Z) Programs include **Dairy Farmer, Growing a Plant, Shopkeeper, Spelling/ Word Finder.**

Football Manager (Addictive Games; Spectrum) Manage your own football team for five years. See page 68.

Homes (Heinemann; Acorn BBC) Five programs on the theme of Homes, including **Central Heating, Home Finances, Town Planning, Spelling/Word Finder.**

Introducing Geography (Acorn BBC Publications; Acorn BBC) Four simulations involving climbing Mount Everest, being a nomad in the Sahara, flying a plane to Los Angeles, surviving a plane crash and escaping down river.

Kon-Tiki (Golem; Acorn BBC) Based on Thor Heyerdahl's Kon-Tiki expedition. Students record on a map the raft's position and enter notes in the logbook on the creatures found, unusual events and storms.

Let's Explore London (Cambridge Software House Ltd; Acorn BBC) Simulation of a journey around London, to be used by groups of students as part of a larger project. The database has over 150 places of interest and the program also allows for teachers to input their own data.

Magnus Connection (BP Educational Services; Acorn BBC; RML) Simulates the computer system used by BP to control the movement of personnel to and from the Magnus oil platform which is situated northeast of Shetland.

Making Ends Meet (Cambridge University Press; Acorn BBC) Designed to give school-leavers insight into personal financial management. All the prices and messages can be updated or changed.

Market Place (MECC; Atari, Commodore 64) Four business simulations. In **Sell Apples** the major objective is to determine the best price based on number sold. **Sell Plants** emphasizes the role of advertising. **Sell Lemonade** simulates a lemonade stand. **Sell Bicycles** deals with the concepts of supply and demand.

Mary Rose (Ginn; Acorn BBC, RM Nimbus) Simulates the raising of the Mary Rose from the seabed in Portsmouth Harbour.

Micros in Business (Acornsoft, Acorn BBC) Five modules: **Personnel** (recruitment, promotion, manpower projects and holiday chart), **Spreadsheet, Word Processor** (a step-by-step introduction), **Database**, and **Planner** (daily records of diary entries).

Moneyplan (Careers Consultants Ltd; Acorn BBC) Personal money management simulation. **PAYSLIP** is an aid to understanding the structure of a payslip. **BUDGET** deals with the forward planning of expenditure. **CREDIT** compares the various forms of instalment credit. Written in conjunction with Lloyds Bank.

Oregon Trail (MECC; Apple) See **Simulations (MECC)**, below

Osprey (Bourne Educational; Acorn BBC, Amstrad 464, Commodore 64) Players are responsible for protecting the precariously small Scottish osprey population against egg-stealers, huntsmen and inquisitive tourists. Ten skill levels.

Paraffin File (BP Educational Service; Acorn BBC, RM Nimbus) Concentrates on the concept of 'marketing mix' with reference to price, advertising and sales staff.

Quick Cartage Company (Jacaranda Wiley; Acorn BBC) Practises map-reading, problem-solving, decision-making and mathematical skills. Each player is in charge of a lorry delivering building supplies.

Running the British Economy (Longman; Acorn BBC, RM Nimbus) Students have to decide on changes in government expenditure, the money supply and tax rates in order to fine tune the economy and eliminate inflationary or deflationary gaps. Difficult stuff.

Sailing Ships Game (Longman; Acorn; Apple) Students navigate a large sailing ship around the oceans, coping with hurricanes, heavy seas and ice.

Simulations (MECC; Apple; Commodore 64; Radio Shack 111/4) **Furs** simulates the fur trade in eastern North America in the 1770s. **The Oregon Trail** simulates a trip by covered wagon from Missouri to Oregon in 1847. **Voyageur** simulates the transportation of furs by canoe in northern Minnesota and southern Ontario in the early 1800s.

Sixgam (Pitmansoft; Acorn BBC) Up to six teams of students act as firms which compete in selling word processors in international markets for up to a decade.

Stokmar (Acornsoft; Acorn BBC) Part of Business Games suite. Groups of students compete, the aim being to increase £1,200 to £5,000 by buying and selling shares.

Teddytronic (Longman; Acorn BBC, RM Nimbus) Students take over the management of a firm producing electronically controlled teddy bears and must make decisions on output, labour and wages, prices and advertising, and loans.

Telemar (Acornsoft; Acorn BBC) Part of **Business Games** suite. Groups of students run a television factory.

Town (Cambridgeshire Software House Ltd; Acorn BBC) Students construct a town plan; they can then print it out and move people around it.

Travel (Heinemann Computers in Education; Acorn BBC) Five programs on the theme of travel. Includes **Car Journey, Ballooning, Special Agent,** (chase a spy across Europe), **Punctuation Practice, Spelling/Word Finder.**

Unisim (Unilever Educational Liaison; Acorn BBC, RM Nimbus) Business simulation for up to 7 teams. Decisions have to be made about production, marketing, selling, finance and planning. Difficult.

Yellow River Kingdom (BBC Publications, Acorn BBC) Students rule over a kingdom, making decisions about disposition of manpower, resources, etc.

Yes, Chancellor (Topologika; Acorn BBC, Nimbus) A serious simulation running the British economy based on a simple but correct model of the problem of raising and using money.

ADVENTURES

Adventure Master (CBS; Apple, Atari, Commodore 64, IBM PC) Authoring package for adventure games.

Adventure Writer (Codewriter Corporation; Atari, Commodore 64, IBM PC) Authoring package for adventure games.

Colossal Adventure (Level 9 Computing; Acorn BBC) Challenging and time-consuming.

Computer Novel Construction Set (Hayden; Apple) Authoring package for adventure games.

Countdown to Doom (Acornsoft; Acorn BBC) Space adventure. A battle against time after forced landing on alien planet with corrosive atmosphere and treasure. Challenging.

Détective, Le (Wida Software; IBM PC) French adventure. Players choose objects to help them chase art thieves.

Felony (CBS; Apple, Commodore 64, IBM PC) Detectives fight a crime wave in the city of Huxley. Up to four players competing with each other. See page 76.

Flash Rogers (unpublished; Acorn BBC) One-lesson adventure. See pages 71-73.

Flowers of Crystal (4Mation; Acorn BBC, RM Nimbus) Save a world from ecological disaster. Audio cassette gives the background: you do the rest. Very good reviews.

Genesis (Dynacomp; Apple) Authoring package for adventure games.

Granny's Garden (4Mation, Acorn BBC) Popular adventure for younger learners.

Hitchhiker's Guide to the Galaxy, The (Infocom; Apple, IBM PC, Macintosh) Manic space adventure based on radio comedy series by Douglas Adams. Difficult.

Hobbit, The (Melbourne House; Acorn BBC, Spectrum) Adventure based on JRR Tolkien's novel. Nice graphics.

Incendie à l'Hôtel (Wida Software; Acorn BBC) French adventure. Learners have to escape from burning hotel by moving from room to room and taking objects.

Last Adventure, The (LTS; Acorn BBC) Authoring package for adventure games. Can be used with a concept keyboard.

London Adventure (British Council/CUP; Acorn BBC, Apple, IBM PC) Multiple-choice adventure for EFL students, set in London. Described on page 75.

Murder by the Dozen (CBS; Apple, Commodore 64, IBM PC) Solve twelve crimes along the lines of **Felony.**

Mystery House (Sierra On-line; Apple) Players explore a large abandoned Victorian house in order to find hidden jewels and discover a murderer. See pages 73-74.

Philosopher's Quest (Acornsoft; Acorn BBC) Treasure-hunting adventure. Challenging.

The Quill (Mirrorsoft; Acorn BBC, Spectrum, Amstrad 464) Authoring package for adventure games.

Spooky Manor (Acornsoft; Acorn BBC). Nice system of four text windows, one for each player. Good maps.

Tombs of Arkenstone (Arnold-Wheaton; Acorn BBC) Supplied with booklets and maps. Allows students to author their own adventures within rather strict limits.

Trésor caché, Le (Wida Software; IBM PC) Treasure hunt for learners of French.

Vol 433 à Destination de Nice (Wida Software, IBM PC) A travel adventure for learners of French.

Wizard and the Princess, The (Sierra On-line; Apple) Typical commercial adventure game with graphics. See p. 70-71.

Your Adventure (LTS; Acorn BBC) Authoring package for adventure games.

INTERACTIVE AUDIO AND VIDEO

Audio Lab (American Language Academy; IBM PC) Plug voice card into PC and perform hear and repeat exercises. Text is displayed on screen and individual items can be highlighted and heard. Has authoring facility.

Autotutor (David Little, unpublished; Acorn BBC, IBM PC) An authoring package enabling the teacher to link computer and VHS videocassette recorder to create Interactive Video exercises.

Back Home (Wida Software; Acorn BBC; Apple, IBM PC, Macintosh) Audio cassette of twelve EFL songs (from Longman), the *Back Home Companion* (comprehension and other classroom activities based on the songs) and computer programs for Cloze, Storyboard and Dictation exercises.

Bid for Power (BBC; Acorn BBC) Videodisc version of the already published Business English materials I.V version by Brighton Polytechnic. See page 83.

Eurocentre Videodisc (unpublished) Consists of two programs: **Getting the Message** and **Danger Mission** plus related library material. (See page 83.)

European Connection, The (IBM UK/BBC/Vektor; IBM PC) An interactive video disk for mature learners of business English.

Expodisc (Ealing College of Higher Education, The Buckinghamshire College) An interactive videodisc for English learners of Business Spanish.

Flight 505 (BBC) An interactive videodisc designed for Japanese businessmen.

MacEnglish (Proficiency; Macintosh) Uses Hypercard-like environment to present and explore text, graphics and high-quality digitised sound. Comes with a sound box and uses compact disks for storage.

Mastwriter (Mast Learning Systems; IBM PC) An authoring package for question and answer activities using the Tandberg AECAL cassette recorder.

Micro Stories (Wida Software; Acorn BBC; Apple, IBM PC, Macintosh) Audio cassette of 24 short stories and anecdotes plus Cloze, Storyboard and Dictation computer programs.

Micro Verse (Wida Software; BBC; Apple) Audio cassette of 24 poems, plus Storyboard, Cloze and Dictation computer programs.

Montevidisco (Brigham Young University) Interactive videodisk for learners of Spanish. Simulates a visit to a Mexican village.

Storyboard Plus (Wida Software; BBC; Apple, IBM PC, Macintosh) Eighteen anecdotes by Andrew Harrison spoken on cassette. Each anecdote is presented as a resumé for Storyboard reconstruction and on the Macintosh and IBM has gap-filling exercises.

Top Class (Format; BBC, IBM PC, RM Nimbus) A general authoring system that intrrfaces with tape-based video and audio as well as CD ROM.

Voicecart (University of Wuppertal/Berndt Rüschoff; IBM) Interactive digital audio system for listening comprehension.

DATABASES

Collins On-Line (Collins; IBM PC) While working with their own word-processor users can access the Collins Bilingual Dictionaries from disk, each with approximately 35,000 translation equivalents. Spanish, English, French, Italian.

Data Handler in the Classroom (MECC; Apple) Designed to teach database concepts.

Factfile (Cambridge University Press; Acorn BBC, Apple) Simple database package in use in many UK primary schools. Teachers' Handbook gives step-by-step instructions on using programs.

General Household Survey (Longman; Acorn BBC) Three discs contain information on poverty, class and gender in Britain taken from the General Household Survey of 1979. Documentation enables the user to follow a short course on the chosen theme, extracting data from the computer at appropriate points.

Harraps Multi-Lingual Dictionary Database (Harraps; IBM PC) While using a word-processing package users can gain rapid access to five million words in eight languages stored on CD ROM.

Lexikon (Tools of the Trade; IBM PC) A memory-resident 23,000 English-German and German-English dictionary. While using a standard word-processor users can look up German equivalents and slot them into the text. Also authoring editor.

Library (Resource Regional Software Service; Acorn BBC) A library book database that children can operate. It holds a large number of records and can search on various keywords.

Linguawrite (Multilingua; IBM PC) A building block translation aid. Stereotyped business phrases are found in a database and automatically translated into or from various European languages, then entered into word processor for polishing. Optional text editor available.

Longman Mini-Concordancer (Longman; IBM PC) A program that enables teachers to input corpora of up to 55,000 words each for research and teaching purposes. Easy-to-use pull down selection menus.

Macroeconomic Database (Longman; Acorn BBC, RM Nimbus) Comprises national income and related data on 25 countries for 1959-81, a suite of statistical programs for manipulating the data and for testing hypotheses and a data manager program which provides an update facility.

Masterfile (Beebugsoft; Acorn BBC) All-purpose database package. Compatible with View and Wordwise.

PC Globe (PC Globe Inc, IBM PC). Users scan through maps of the whole world, zoom in on chosen continents, countries, cities, and call up statistical data about each. Updated annually.

PFS FILE and **PFS REPORT** (Scholastic; Apple) **PFS FILE** is a simple database package; **PFS REPORT** prepares printed reports in the form of columns using data files created with **PFS FILE**.

Picfile (Cambridge University Press; Acorn BBC) Uses datafiles created by **Factfile** and allows students to make pictorial representations of the information. The data may be displayed as a count graph (bar chart), cumulative count graph or scattergram. Includes sample files.

Regional Statistics (Longman; Acorn BBC) Covers population, occupations, income levels, housing tenure and the ownership of consumer durables.

Viewbook (Information Education, Acorn BBC, IBM PC). Established topic books transferred to disk. Geography, history, environment – even Shakespeare. Users can turn pages but also perform mini-concordances and searches and even edit. Optional authoring facility.

Where in the World is Carmen Sandiego? (Brøderbund Software; Apple, IBM PC, Macintosh) A graphics and text detective game in which players have to travel the world chasing a band of art thieves. Comes with almanac and teacher packs. Also **Where in Europe, USA, in Time...?**

Useful addresses

Acornsoft Ltd., c/o Vector Service, 13 Dennington Road, Wellingborough, Northants

Aldoda International, 27 Elizabeth Mews, London NW3 4UH

American Language Academy Suite 200 11426 Rockville Pike, Rockville Maryland 20852 USA

Arnold-Wheaton Ltd, Parkside Lane, Leeds LS11 5T

AVP Computing, (Educational Software catalogue house) School Hill Centre, Chepstow, Gwent NP6 5PH.

BBC Publications, 35, Marylebone High St, London W1M 4AA.

Beebugsoft, PO Box 50, St Albans, Herts.

Bell Educational Trust, South Road, Saffron Walden, CB11 3DP

BP Educational Service, PO Box 5, Wetherby, W. Yorks LS23 7GH.

British Council, 10, Spring Gardens, London SW1A 2BN.

Brøderbund Software Inc., 17 Paul Drive, San Rafael, CA 94903-2101, USA

Cambridge Language Arts Software Ltd., 2, Howard Court, Howard Road, Cambridge, CB5 8RB

Cambridge University Press, The Edinburgh Building, Shaftesbury Road, Cambridge CB2 2RU

Cambridgeshire Software House Ltd, Town Hall, St Ives, Huntingdon, Cambridgeshire PE17 4AL.

Camsoft, (developer and catalogue house) 10, Wheatfield Close, Maidenhead, Berks SL6 3PS.

CBS Software, 1, Fawcett Place, Greenwich CT 06386 USA

Centre for Information on Language Teaching, Regent's College, Inner Circle, Regent's Park, London NW1 4NS.

Chalksoft Ltd., PO Box 49, Spalding, Lincs, PE11 1NZ.

Collins Educational, Freepost, Glasgow G4 OYX.

Computer Concepts, 16 Wayside, Chipperfield, Herts WD4 9JJ 5FB.

Davidson and Associates Inc. 3135 Kashiwa St., Torrance, CA 90505 USA

DesignWare, 185 Berry St, San Francisco, CA 94107 USA

DMA Computers, 26 Clare Street, Dublin 2, Ireland

Dynacomp Inc., 1064 Gravel Road, Webster, NY 14580 USA

4Mation Educational Resources, Linden Lea, Rock Park, Barnstaple, Devon EX32 9AQ.

ESM, Duke Street, Wisbech, Cambs PE13 2AE

Eurocentres Learning Service, Seestrasse 247, CH 8038 Zurich, Switzerland

Fisher-Marriot Software, 3 Grove Road, Anstey CV7 9JD

Format pc, Goods Wharf, Goods Road, Belper, DE5 1UU, UK

Gessler Educational Software Inc, 55 West 13th St, New York City, NY 10011 USA

Ginn & Co Ltd, Prebendal House, Parson's Fee, Aylesbury, Bucks.

Griffin and George, 285 Ealing Road, Alperton, Wembley, Middlesex HA0 1HJ.

Hayden Software Company Inc., 600 Suffolk Street, Lowell, MA 01854 USA

HRM Software, 175, Tompkins Avenue, Pleasantville, NY 10570 USA

ILECC (Inner London Educational Computing Centre) John Ruskin Street, London Se5 0PQ

Information Education Ltd, Unit 33, The Enterprise Centre, Bedford St., Stoke-on-Trent, ST1 4BR

Intellectual Software c/o Queue, Inc (catalogue house) 562 Boston Avenue, Bridgeport, CT 06610, USA

Jacaranda Wiley Software, Baffins Lane, Chichester, Sussex PO19 1UD.

Leisure Genius c/o Virgin Mastertronic International Inc. 18001 Cowan, Irvine, CA 92714 USA

Living Videotext, 2432 Charleston Rd, Mountain View, CA 94043.

Locheesoft Ltd, Oak Villa, New Alyth, Perthshire, PH11 8NN, Scotland.

Longman ELT Software, Burnt Mill, Harlow, Essex CM20 2JE

Macmillan Education Limited, Houndmills, Basingstoke, Hampshire RG21 2XS

McGraw Hill Book Co, Software Support Service, Shoppenhangers Rd, Maidenhead, Berks, SL6 2QL

MECC (Minnesota Educational Computing Corporation), 3490 Lexington Ave. Nth, St Paul, Minnesota 55112.

MicroTac Software, 4655 Cass St., Suite 304, San Diego, CA 92109 USA

Milliken Publishing Company, 1100 Research Boulevard, PO Box 2157, St Louis MO63132

Multilingua, 61 Chiswick Staithe, Hartington Road, London W4 3TP

NCET (National Centre for Educational Technology) Sir Williams Lyons Rd, Science Park, University of Warwick, Coventry, CV4 7EZ

Owl International, Guide Distribution, 497 Battersea Park Road, Battersea, London SW11 4LW

Oxford University Press, Walton St, Oxford, OX2 6DP

PC Globe 4435 South Rural Road, Building 5, Suite 333, Tempe, Arizona 85282, USA

Palmsoft, Abo Academi, PO Box 311, SF 65101 Vaasa, Finland

Pitmansoft, Pitman Publishing, Southport PR9 9YF.

Precision Software, 4, Park Terrace, Worcester Park, Surrey, KT4 7JZ.

Proficiency, 185 South State St, Suite 850, Salt Lake City, Utah 84111, USA

Question Mark Computing, 12 Heath Villas, Vale of Health, London NW3 1AW

Resource Regional Software Service, S. Yorks and Humberside RIC, Exeter Road, Off Coventry Grove, Doncaster, DN2 4PY.

Research Machines Ltd, Mill St, Oxford OX2 0BW

Rickett Educational Media (educational software catalogue house) Ilton, Ilminster, Somerset TA19 9HS

Scarborough Systems, Inc., 25, North Broadway, Tarrytown, NY 10591 USA.

Scholastic Software, 730 Bway, 9th Floor, NYC 10003 USA

147

Sierra On-Line Inc., Sierra On-Line Building, Coarsegold, CA93614.

SoftKat (catalogue house) 20630 Nordhoff St, Chatsworth, CA 91311

Softmill Torpankuja 5 C 16 SF 40740 Jyväskylä Finland

Studentlitteratur, Box 141, 221 00 Lund, Sweden.

Sunburst Software, 39 Washington Avenue, Pleasantville, New York 10570.

Tandberg International, 7 Hales Road, Leeds LS12 4PL

Tedimen Software, PO Box 23, Southampton SO9 7BD

Tools of the Trade, 129 Sherwood Place, Lethbridge, Alberta, Canada T1K 6G6

Training Agency, Moorfoot, Sheffield S1 4PQ

Unilever Educational Liaison, PO Box 68, Unilever House, Blackfriars, London EC4P 4BQ

Wida Software Ltd, (developer and catalogue house) 2 Nicholas Gardens, London W5 5HY

Magazines and journals

Athelstan News PO Box 8025, La Jolla, Ca 92038-8025 USA: Ed Michael Barlow

British Journal of Educational Technology: Council for Educational Technology, 3, Devonshire Street, London W1N 2BA

CALL Austria: Many interesting and detailed articles in English and German on Austrian CALL practice in the classroom. Ed. Günter Schmid, Unterer Schreiberweg, 1190 Vienna, Austria

CAELL Journal (Computer Assisted English Language Learning): Norman Johnson, ISTE, University of Oregon, 1878 Agate St., Eugene, Oregon 97403, USA

CALL-IF: Institut für Angewandte Sprachen, Rostock University, Germany: Ed. Dr Edith Buchholz.

CALL-IS Newsletter: (Dept of English Language and Literature, University of Toledo, Ohio, OH 43606-3390, USA). TESOL newsletter not confined to MSDOS machines. Ed. Doug Johnson.

Calico Journal (Computer Assisted Language Learning and Instruction Consortium), Brigham Young University, Provo, Utah 84062, USA

Callboard: Newsletter on Computer Assisted Language Learning, Ealing College of Higher Education, 1 The Grove, London W5 5DX. ed. Graham Davies.

Educational Computing, Priory Court, 30-32 Farringdon Lane, London EC1R 3AU. Deals with computers and education in general but some articles and advertisements are of interest to language teachers.

Electric Word, Emmalaan 21- EW 17, 1075 AT Amsterdam, The Netherlands

MSDOS Users' Group Newsletter, Sultan Qaboos University, Oman. CALL Interest Section newsletter of TESOL (Teachers of English to Speakers of Other Languages). Ed. Vance Stevens.

MUESLI News: (Newsletter of IATEFL special interest group, Microcomputer Users in English as a Second Language Institutions) but not restricted to English teaching. Much useful and practical information. Four issues a year mailed to members of International Association of Teachers of English as a Foreign Language. IATEFL, 3 Kingsdown Chambers, Kingsdown Park, Tankerton, Whitstable, Kent CT 2DJ, UK

On-CALL: Language Centre, Bond University, Gold Coast, Queensland 4229, Australia. Ed. Mike Levy.

ReCALL: CTI, Centre for Modern Languages, University of Hull, HU6 7RX, UK

SYSTEM (International Journal of Educational Technology and Language Learning Systems), Pergamon Press, Headington Hill Hall, Oxford OX3 0BW

Times Educational Supplement, PO Box 7, 200 Gray's Inn Road, London WC1X 8EZ. (Frequent EFL and CAL supplements.)

User groups

These are usually associations of users of particular computer types, Apple Users, BBC users, etc. Whether organised by the manufacturers or independent, whether strictly amateur or with a commercial bent, all are useful. The list below is a small selection of groups and their newsletters. Other addresses are printed regularly in the computer magazines.

Acorn User (for BBC B users; 12 issues per annum) Redwood Publishing, 68, Long Acre, London WC2E 9JH

Beebug (for BBC micro users; 10 issues per annum) PO Box 109, High Wycombe, Bucks.

Mac Times: Newsletter of the Mac User Group. Monthly.

Research Machines National User Group, c/o Research Machines, PO Box 75, Oxford, OX2 0BV. (4 magazines pa)

Bibliography

A specialised bibliography on computer-assisted language learning (No. B32) is available from the Centre for Information on Language Teaching. The following is a selective list of the most recent publications and also includes other books mentioned in the text.

AHMAD K, CORBETT, G, ROGERS, M and SUSSEX, R *Computers, Language Learning and Language Teaching* (Cambridge University Press, 1985)

BARLOW, M *Working with Computers* (Athelstan Press, 1989)

BERER, M and RINVOLUCRI, M *Mazes: A Problem-Solving Reader* (Heinemann, 1985)

CHANDLER, D *Exploring English with Microcomputers* (Microelectronics Programme/Centre for Educational Technology, 1983)

CHANDLER, D *Computers and Literacy* (Open University Press, 1985)

COUNCIL FOR EDUCATIONAL TECHNOLOGY *A Guide to the Selection of Microcomputers* (CET, 1980)

DAVIES, G D AND HIGGINS, J *The Use of Computers in Language Learning: A Teacher's Guide* (Centre for Information on Language Teaching and Research, 1985) Out of print.

DAVIES, G D *Talking BASIC: An Introduction to BASIC Programming for Users of Language* (Cassell Computing, 1985) out of print.

FOX J, MATTHEWS, A and C, ROPE, A *Educational Technology in Modern Language Learning* (University of East Anglia and the Bell Educational Trust for The Training Agency 1990)

FARTHING, J *Business Mazes* (Hart-Davis 1981)

HARDISTY, D and WINDEATT, S *CALL* (OUP, 1990)

HEWER, S *Making the most of IT Skills* (CILT, Technology in Language Learning, 1989)

HIGGINS, J *Language Learners and Computers* (Longman 1988)

HIGGINS, J and JOHNS, T *Computers in Language Learning* (Collins Educational, 1984)

JONES, C and FORTESCUE, S *Using Computers in the Language Classroom* (Longman, 1986, revised 1990).

KENNING, M J and M M *An Introduction to Computer Assisted Language Teaching* (Oxford University Press, 1983)

LAST, R *Language Teaching and the Micro Computer* (Blackwell, 1984)

LAST, R W and JOHNSTON, I *Language Teaching Software for the BBC Micro: A Programming Guide for the Non-Scientist* (Blackwell, 1985)

LEECH, G and CANDLIN, C (eds.) *Computers and the English Language* (Longman, 1985)

LEVY, M and FARRUGIA, D *Computers in Language Teaching: Analysis, Research and Reviews* (Footscray College of TAFE, 1988)

KECSKÉS, I and AGÓCS, L (eds.) *New Tendencies in Computer Assisted Language Learning* (Kossuth University, Debrecen, Hungary, 1989)

PAPERT, S *Mindstorms* (Harvester Press Ltd, 1980)

RÜNF, B *Fremdsprachenunterricht mit computergestützten Materialien* (Max Hueber-Verlag, 1986)

PENNINGTON, M C (ed.) *Teaching Languages with Computers: the State of the Art* (Athelstan, 1989)

TRIBBLE, C and JONES, G *Using Concordances in the Language Classroom* (Longman, 1990)

WYATT, D H *Computers and ESL* (Harcourt, Brace Jovanovich, 1984)

Glossary of CALL expressions

adapted cloze tests See cloze tests.

authoring language A simplified version of a programming language. The user has to learn the commands before he can write a program. Microtext and Pilot are authoring languages for the BBC and Apple computers respectively.

authoring package A program framework which allows users to enter the data they wish the program to use.

CALL Computer-assisted language learning.

cloze tests Tests of reading skill in which words are deleted from a text at regular intervals. Students have to fill in the spaces with appropriate words. In computer-directed generative cloze tests students can choose the frequency with which words are deleted; in computer-directed adapted cloze tests the teacher decides which words or parts of words are to be deleted, often focusing on a specific grammatical point such as prepositions or a specific vocabulary point and allowing for alternative possibilities.

compact discs These are now used for audio recordings since they are less easily damaged and produce recordings of higher quality than long playing records. They are increasingly used for storing computer programs since they are capable of storing an immense amount of information, far more even than is currently possible even on a hard disc. They are also being linked up to a computer to provide an audio component, the advantage over audio cassettes being the much faster access time and immunity to such problems as tape stretch.

computer display panel A system whereby the screen display, instead of being sent to a monitor which only two or three users can observe in comfort, is sent to a large screen often via an overhead projector. Essential for displays to large audiences.

dash map A help function for students whereby the computer produces an outline of the word using dashes. Sometimes in addition the student's correct input is displayed, thus co − − u − er would be a dash map for the word **computer.**

interactive video A video recorder is linked to a computer enabling the students to see and hear video extracts linked to computer exercises. For example, the students may see a short video extract of two people discussing the best way to get to a restaurant. They then see a map of the area and use the cursor to follow the directions and get to the restaurant. The computer analyses their input and, if they make a mistake, plays the relevant extract from the conversation again. Either a video cassette or a laserdisc recorder can be used but the latter offers far more rapid and accurate access to sections of the video.

speech digitiser This is a device which is usually a microphone linked to a card that plugs into the computer and enables sound to be processed electronically. Unlike **speech synthesis** – see below – the sound quality is near-perfect and increasing use is being made of it in language work. Because this system uses up very large amounts of storage memory digitised sound is most often stored on compact or laser discs.

speech synthesis A system whereby the computer can produce a more or less human-like voice. Various systems are on the market, some better than others but none are of the quality desirable for language teaching.

text mutilation The deleting, by the computer, of parts or all of a text.

text reconstruction The reconstruction by the student of a text held in the computer's memory.

voice recognition The ability of the computer to understand information given orally. Still in its infancy.

Index

Names of programs appear in bold. Books are in italic. See also useful addresses, magazines and journals, bibliography and CALL glossary.